M

Haram
Vigra • Torholmen
Erkna • • Søvik
Godøy • • • Bjørgeholmen
Fiskarstrand • • ÅLESUND
Kvalsvik • Remøy • Solavågen
Skorpa • • Leinøy
Fosnavåg • • Ulsteinvik

Sunn

• Volda

Søre Sunnmøre

Bremangerlandet   *Nordfjord*
Torvanger • • Bremanger
Nordbotnen • • Svelgen
Hovden • • Øvrebotnen
• Domba

Florø • • Jølster

Sunnfjord

SOGN AND FJORDANE

Alden • Atløy
Bulandet • • Askvoll
• Værlandet

Sogn

Hyllestad

Solund   *Sognefjorden*

Masfjorden

Fedje • • Andvik
Hernar • Skageneset
Sture • • Lygra • Bjørsvik
Øygarden • Manger   • Voss
Rong • • Osterøy
Askøy • Frekhaug
Davanger •
Hauglandshella • • BERGEN   HORDALAND
Sotra • Fjøsanger
Telavåg • • Kjokkarvik   *Hardanger*
Steinsland • • Os
Kalve • • Bakkasund

Sunnhordland

Urangsvåg
Øklandsvågen
Stavland
Finnås • Rubbestadneset
Nesse • • Svortland
Melingsvågen • Oldereide
Sønstebøvågen   *Bømlo*

Espevær •

HAUGESUND ●

• Jelsa

Kopervik •
Karmøy

Skudeneshavn • ROGALAND

STAVANGER ●

NORWAY

NORTH
SEA

KRISTIANSAND ●

Shetland Bus

Text and photos
Trygve Sørvaag

Translated by

Deborah Miller

Shetland Bus

© The Shetland Times Ltd, Lerwick, 2002.

ISBN 1 898852 88 X

British Library Cataloguing-in-Publication Data.
A catalogue for this book is available from the British Library.

Published by The Shetland Times Ltd, Gremista, Lerwick, Shetland, Scotland. ZE1 0PX

Printed in Finland.

Design and layout: Kjersti Hjelmeland Brakstad, Bergen.
Map: Sverre Mo, Bergen.

Original title: Englandsfeber
Copyright 2002 by Trygve Sørvaag

Published by agreement with Eide forlag, Bergen 2002.

Contents :

Foreword

The idea for this book came about as I completed a photography project in Shetland in April 1999. Having some extra time, I sought out nine Shetlanders who remembered the wartime traffic between Norway and Shetland. As a result of these encounters, I was drawn into the mystique that surrounds the North Sea Traffic.

The stories of Shetlands-Larsen and the Shetland Bus have been a source of fascination for several generations. Now it was my turn to be gripped by these exciting real-life events – a heroism and courage with which no novel can compete. I became so caught up in the stories that I decided to hunt for clues. Clues that could reveal something of the legend and the people involved in this extraordinary traffic.

Three years later, I have met more than one hundred people on both sides of the North Sea. Time after time I have stood face-to-face with the ordinary people who are never mentioned in history books.

The encounters have resulted in over one hundred hours of tape recordings, 7000 photographs, and this book, which has received the title "Shetland Bus - Faces and Places 60 Years On". In this book we meet again the coastal folk who, in some way or another, were touched by or met the individuals and the boats David Howarth wrote about in his best-selling book "The Shetland Bus".

Rather than present a comprehensive portrait of the North Sea Traffic, something already brilliantly accomplished by others, this book takes a different tack by turning the spotlight on ordinary people.

The objective was to provide a documentary about these figures – coastal dwellers who created war history. Unexpectedly, the project became something much more. I suddenly realised that I – the narrator – had become part of the story. The more people I interviewed, the more it became clear that there were still many unanswered questions. I could help to track down some of these answers. I had met the rescuers, and I had met the rescued. I had met those who owned fishing boats, and those who stole them. I had met those who helped and those who had received help. They themselves had not set eyes upon each other since that fateful night or day sixty years earlier. For two generations they had wondered about each other. Not knowing who each other were or how things had gone for each other. Now I could complete the stories – their stories.

In this book it is the participants who hold centre stage. They present their stories themselves. It is possible that in some instances their memories may play tricks on them, but this is how events crystallize for them. Sixty years on, they have become part of our history. Regardless, I have invested a significant amount of effort into relating the stories as accurately as possible.

Paring the often elaborate narratives down to the short accounts presented in this book has proved a laborious and painful process. Many of the accounts are worthy of an entire book. It is also possible that the sources would have emphasised completely different sides of their stories if they had been able to choose themselves, and some may feel that I have not been just with them. Yet it is these aspects of their stories that captivated me – and that I will share with you.

Most of the interviews were conducted in the spring and summer of 2000, and each story takes as its starting point the situations in which I met the subjects. Since this time their lives may have changed dramatically, and I know that many of the people we meet in these pages will never view the final results.

The individuals in this book are only a selection of the one hundred people I interviewed. This does not mean that the 25 people not included here are less important. Also their contributions have been vital to the construction of a well-rounded picture of the topic. All of the material collected will be preserved by the Norwegian North Sea Traffic Museum in Telavåg. There it will assume its place as part of the museum's documentation of our past.

This collaboration with the North Sea Traffic Museum is not only due to the fact that it is the leading museum and competence centre for this aspect of our history, but also because "Shetland Bus – Faces and Places 60 Years On" is the result of a close and productive co-operation with the museum, from the book's inception to its completion. Without the practical support, helpful counsel, and constructive criticism of Museum Director Egil Christophersen and Educational Supervisor Jenny Heggvik, the creation of this book would have proved an arduous and solitary task.

In my work I have been greatly assisted by the books of Ragnar Ulstein, David Howarth, and James W. Irvine. Many individuals and institutions have provided inestimable help – so many that it would be impossible to list all of them. I will instead extend my thanks to each and every one of them – especially to all the people I have met during my travels. I would nevertheless like to express particular thanks to Svein Carl Sivertsen, Trine Andersen, Kjersti Hjelmeland Brakstad, and José Resinente. However, none of these individuals bears responsibility for any mistakes or omissions that may occur in this book.

Trygve Sørvaag
London/Telavåg, September 2002

A Strange Journey

From Karmøy to Haram.
From London to Unst.
Sixty years after the first Norwegians made the England Crossing,
I began a journey through three countries and four Norwegian counties.
Seven thousand kilometres to meet two coastal communities divided by war,
yet bound together by the same sea. A journey equal to the distance
between Bergen and Bombay.

An Encounter with a Legend

They turned every stone,
but they forgot the house on the islet.
The marks of the drama of 1943 are gone,
but the mystique still permeates the tiny island.
Here Shetlands-Larsen and his men sought shelter
after one of the most dramatic shipwrecks of the
North Sea Traffic.

Torholmen in Haram, Møre and Romsdal

In the Wake of a Funeral

The Shetland Bus steered by the light in the window.
They were hidden by the bay as they waited for night.
Without a word, the passengers climbed on board.
The last rocks slid by.
Since then no one has heard a sound.
The *Blia* sank – without a trace.
43 people vanished that night.

Bømlo, Hordaland

The North Sea Link

It's when times get tough that we really know our friends; this applies to nations as well as to individuals. The last world war brought immense suffering to vast parts of Europe and was an onerous time for our countries. Norway was occupied and Great Britain fought long alone against Nazi tyranny. Great Britain opened its doors for Norwegian exiles: the king, the government, and thousands of ordinary women and men. For their part, the exiled Norwegians did what they could to support Norway and Great Britain's common battle and the allied victory.

The close relationship between our countries can only be appreciated against its background of extensive historical development. With the North Sea as our link, cultural impulses were exchanged and economic co-operation fostered, generation after generation. During World War II, the North Sea became more than a link between our two peoples – it became a lifeline.

This book offers an encounter with many of those who, at risk of their own lives, held this lifeline intact. Yet this book is not merely a vital documentation of what these people did; it is also a tribute to their deeds and sacrifices. May it inspire all those who in their daily endeavours maintain contact between our nations, and may it serve to further fortify this contact.

Kjell Magne Bondevik
Prime Minister of Norway

Dangerous Liaisons
The North Sea Traffic 1940-45
By Egil Christophersen, Norwegian North Sea Traffic Museum

Since time immemorial, long before the births of the nations of Great Britain and Norway, the North Sea has served to connect the coastal populations dwelling along its shores. During World War II, this connection became a lifeline between occupied Norway and free Great Britain. The North Sea provided an escape valve for thousands of Norwegians, and supported a vital supply line of people and materials crucial to the build-up of military resistance in occupied Norway. This lifeline was maintained by the manifold contributions of countless women and men. Rarely has one seen such selfless effort; many of these individuals ended in watery graves or fell to the occupier's bullets.

What we here discuss – the North Sea Traffic – was both civilian and military. It began as an unorganised enterprise in which people crossed the North Sea by their own devices. By the time this first wave of crossings ended towards the close of 1941, traffic over the North Sea had assumed an organised military fashion involving the shuttling of agents and military equipment from Great Britain, primarily the Shetland Islands, to the Norwegian coast, and exiles back from Norway.

The England Crossing

Six men and a woman photographed on board the Klegg. They left Ålesund on 28th August 1941, and arrived in Shetland on 1st September, where this picture was taken. The half-open motorboat was one of the smallest used in the England crossing.

Already in the spring and early summer of 1940, the first boats set sail for Great Britain, or England, as people then said. This was the beginning of the England Crossing, the first phase of the North Sea Traffic. Those who left were mainly young, unmarried men. Many had already fought against the Germans in Norway, and they now wished to join forces with what they hoped would be a British invasion of Norway to expel the occupiers. It is said of these individuals that they fled to the war. Most crossed in fishing vessels of various types, and there were also those who made the journey in small cabin cruisers, sailboats, rowboats, etc. Nor was the North Sea at its worst at this time of year. As it gradually became clear that the battle to free Norway would be a protracted one, many left the country in order to join the Norwegian military forces being built up in Great Britain.

In the long run, the majority of those who crossed the North Sea did so with the aim of joining the Norwegian army, navy, and air force divisions being established outside the country's borders. Yet as resistance organisations grew in number and extent, they often formed so-called export groups.

The England Crossing in four phases:
On 24th August 1941, the Eva set out from Os in Hordaland with eleven people on board. They enjoyed a meal before departing. As can plainly be seen in the photographs, the journey enjoyed good weather, but due to engine trouble the boat did not arrive in Shetland until 27th August.

The resistance movement developed a network of individuals whose responsibility was to help people out of Norway. In eastern Norway, the export route led primarily to Sweden, while along the west coast, most routes were directed towards Shetland, the closest shore.

Escape and the journey

Norwegian refugees set foot on British soil in Scalloway, Shetland.

An export group might be called upon to help someone out of the country for various reasons. A resistance group might be «fumbling in the dark», in that it lacked contact with Norwegian authorities or with others involved in resistance activities. Someone was therefore usually sent to England to establish contact with the Norwegian authorities, and, if all went well, this person would return with codes and schedules for radio contact. As a result, the Norwegian resistance movement became a playing piece in the great war against Germany.

Nevertheless, most of those assisted by the export groups were people who had to leave because they had come under the scrutiny of the German secret police, the Gestapo. Nor was it always enough that only the individual

They didn't want to work for the Germans. Many crossed the North Sea in order to avoid German service, something that became increasingly militarised during the course of the war.

directly concerned escaped. Often spouses and children had to leave to be on the safe side. It was not uncommon for the Germans to take hostages.

The export groups had to work in total secrecy. The escape was normally organised in phases, often involving diversionary manoeuvres. He or she who was to leave would receive a message with instructions to meet up at a particular place, and to look for a woman or a man with a distinguishing feature. Contact made, the individual was conveyed to a secret apartment where several other refugees might be located. The refugees were then told to take a shuttle boat to a specific place in the archipelago, and to look for a new contact person on the pier there.

When contact was established with this new person, the refugees were transferred to a new hiding place to wait until conditions were right for the crossing. This wait could be a matter of hours or days, or it could stretch out into weeks before the last link in the chain, the skipper in the fishing boat, could set his course westward. The weather could not be appeased, and there was little to be done if the Germans or their collaborators became too inquisitive. One finds several examples in the England Crossing of catastrophe due to over-confidence or carelessness. The delay could be a heavy psychological strain for those who, day after day, lay waiting in an attic or a barn for something to happen. The nature of the crossing could vary. For some it proceeded smoothly, even in smaller vessels. Others had the Gestapo on their heels right up to the moment they pulled away from shore, while still others barely escaped the heaving sea. Boats could arrive in Shetland looking

Almost 300 Norwegian fishing boats came to Great Britain during the war. Many were sent to the little harbour village of Buckie in northern Scotland, where this picture was taken. In Buckie, the boats were overhauled and repaired before being put into various types of service.

like wreckage debris after clashes with the North Sea. Further, one can imagine the appearance of cabins and holds where refugees had struggled in vain for days against seasickness. Some had to turn back, not completing the journey until the following year. At worst, one didn't make it over at all. This could be difficult to accept, especially for those strongly motivated to make a contribution.

On British soil

Setting foot on British soil was a thrilling experience for most of the refugees. Not just because they had made it, or because they had come to a free country, but because Great Britain held a special place in people's hearts at that time. From the summer of 1940, until the Soviet Union joined the war the following summer, Great Britain was the only free European nation at war with Germany. This evoked immense admiration from most Norwegians, replacing the disappointment many had felt regarding the half-hearted British effort during the invasion of Norway. They

The Giske family had to flee Bjørgeholmen in Sunnmøre when it began to «burn under their feet» in the spring of 1945. Here they have reached their destination – Shetland – after passage on the Hitra.

felt they were fortunate to be able to do battle shoulder-to-shoulder with the British.

Upon debarking in Shetland, the refugees were required to follow a set routine. First came a brief interview at the point of arrival, usually Lerwick in Shetland. Afterwards, they were sent to the

Royal Victoria Patriotic School in Wandsworth in south London. Here the intelligence service carried out a long and exhaustive interview, the goal of which was to detect possible German spies among the refugees as well as to gather as much information as possible about Norway. From here one was assigned to the army, navy, air force, or other branches of the service.

A Norwegian refugee family in their new home in London. They have already begun to adopt British ways, but the Norwegian flag is in its rightful place in the family home of Bernt and Samulene Larsen.

Mutual admiration and respect seem to mark an encounter between a London policeman and a young refugee from Lofoten. Note that the policeman has exchanged his customary headgear for a helmet due to the bombing attacks.

If setting foot on British soil was stirring, arriving in London was almost indescribable. Even during the ration years of the war it took the breath from most, and especially from those who had scarcely been away from their small communities in the sea. Those who arrived in London during the *Blitz*, the German bombing in the autumn of 1940, will never forget the scenes. The greater part of the German air force took part in these attacks, and before long entire neighbourhoods of the British capital lay in ruins. In underground stations, people lay pressed together night after night, bombs dropping over them. The refugees were a long way from home, in more than one sense.

During the bombing of London in the autumn of 1940, London Underground stations were used as air-raid shelters.

In time, the number of in Great Britain had increased so considerably that a Norwegian school was established. First located in London, because of the heavy bombing, teachers and students were transferred to Glasgow in 1941. In the summer of 1942, the Norwegian school relocated to a castle outside Aberdeen. Klara Værøyvik (Nybø) from Værlandet was one of the teachers at Drumtochty Castle. Here she is with then Crown Prince Olav and the Minister of Education, Nils Hjelmtveit.

A western Norway phenomenon

In 1940, fifty-six boats departed for Great Britain, carrying 548 people. Most left in May, after the fighting in southern Norway had ended. The subsequent year, 191 boats and 2388 people left. That year most made the journey in August and September, before the autumn storms set in and under cover of the steadily lengthening autumn darkness. This was the best time. 1941 was the major year of the England Crossing; from then on it ebbed away. In 1942 only 17 boats left. The Germans had sharpened their surveillance

Four brothers: three from the foreign front, one from the home front, photographed in Ålesund after the war. From the left: Peder S. Godø (Shetland Bus), Hans S. Vang (Army), Martin S. Godø (Home Forces), and Johan S. Godø (Navy).

Most who left over the North Sea were from the coastal regions of western Norway – for example, Mælandsvågen on Bømlo. The island group in Sunnhordland was one of the chief export points.

and counter-measures considerably, and it had become increasingly difficult to obtain boats. In all, it is believed that a pproximately 3300 indi viduals set sail from the Norwegian coast during the England Crossing, on roughly 300 craft.

Three Norwegian counties stood out during the England Crossing: Hordaland, Sogn and Fjordane, and Møre and Romsdal. In 1940 and 1941 only a handful of boats came from the regions north of Møre and Romsdal. In 1940 the same was true for the region south of Hordaland, while this number rose to 25 in 1941. We can see that the England Crossing was primarily a western Norway phenomenon, mainly limited to the area between Haugesund and Ålesund.

If we look closer at the material, we find that most of those who left were from the perimeter regions of western Norway: the islands and the coasts furthest out in the sea. In other words, those who made the crossing were chiefly recruited from people involved in fishing and seafaring, something that was hardly surprising. These individuals were well-acquainted with the North Sea, and many of them had boats or knew someone who had a boat that could serve the purpose. Consequently, it was fishing boats of various types, for the most part cutters and smacks, that predominated in the England Crossing.

Also unsurprising, as mentioned earlier, is the fact that it was primarily young, unmarried men who left. The soldier life has traditionally been an occupation for young men unfettered by parental responsibilities. This made it easier to break out and leave their communities. Furthermore, if love for one's country wasn't more intense among young men, adventurousness and daring was. Only ten percent of those who left for England were women.

Those who crossed the North Sea hailed from virtually the entire west coast, but some communities were especially notable. Vigra in Møre and Romsdal County and Telavåg in Hordaland County were two of these. From Vigra, between 70 and 80 people left an area with a population of only 1200 people. From Telavåg in Sotra, around 50 youths from a population of about 400 left. It is a recognised phenomenon that when one individual in a locality leads, many follow. This is most likely the case here.

Boats, too, departed from almost every district along the coast, but also here some districts stood out. From both Ålesund in Møre and Romsdal and Bømlo in Sunnhordland twenty-five boats departed; almost twice as many as the next district on the list. Moreover, if we broaden our perspective a little and look at naturally uninterrupted regions across district borders, we discover that the region from Askvoll to Solund served as a centre for the exodus from Sogn and Fjordane, in the same way that Sotra/Øygarden was the export centre for Midthordland.

The enemy took – and the sea took

The enemy and the weather were the chief threats for those crossing the North Sea. The Germans patrolled the north coast with both air and sea craft, and in February 1941, the death penalty was instituted for contact with the enemy. On 26th September 1941, the death penalty was extended to include anyone attempting to leave for England. Aided by their Norwegian sympathisers, the Gestapo and its intelligence organisation Abwehr did all they could to infiltrate the groups involved in the traffic in order to expose and dismantle them. They also hoped through this infiltration to introduce their agents into the flow of refugees entering England. It was therefore not without grounds that Norwegian refugees were thoroughly processed upon arrival. If one looks at the entire North Sea Traffic, it is believed that 121 people were captured by the Germans before or during the crossing. Of these, 51 were executed and nine died in

No one should doubt the risks incurred by those who set their courses westward: «Contact with the enemy punishable by death»

The Germans utilised a variety of means to stop the passage over the North Sea. This was one of them: Parents were seized as hostages for sons and daughters who had left the country.

Even for the experienced seaman or fisherman who transported refugees in one direction and agents in the other, the North Sea could present serious challenges in the dark time of the year.

Artist Ants Lepson's rendition of the sinking of the Blia. The boat went down on 11th November, 1941, with 43 people on board. It was the greatest loss of the North Sea Traffic

captivity. Many others were executed or imprisoned for having participated in organising the traffic.

Yet it was not the enemy that presented the severest dangers to the traffic, but the weather conditions in the North Sea. Almost none of the craft used were designed for such demanding journeys, and when the autumn and winter storms set in these boats encountered major problems. It is estimated that the sea took 160 people, from refugees in rowboats to those travelling in large cutters. The worst period was the autumn of 1941 when several boats went down, including the *Blia,* which vanished while en route from Øklandsvågen to Shetland in November 1941 with 43 people on board. It was the greatest loss of the North Sea Traffic.

Crew and agents on the Arthur photographed before their trip from Lunna to Norway in February of 1942. The crew from the left: Leif Larsen Kinn (back), Kåre Iversen, Leif Larsen (captain), and Palmer Bjørnøy in the wheelhouse. The man in the light-coloured jacket, Bjørn Rørholdt, was to establish a radio station in the Trondheim region, together with the two other agents to the right in the picture.

In the service of the allies

Not only in Norway did sea transport gradually become better organised, the same occurred in Great Britain. Already in the summer of 1940, British authorities realised the military potential of the refugees and their boats. In addition to being skilful sailors, the refugees were intimately familiar with the Norwegian seaboard, and their boats had the advantage of being able to easily blend in with the fishing boats along the shoreline. Such advantages were not available to British vessels, crew, or leadership. Consequently, several skippers were asked by the British authorities if they would be willing to take agents and equipment to selected sites along the Norwegian coast. The goal was

Some of the Shetland Bus's boats at the base in Scalloway.

A legend photographed at a 40-year interval. Shetlands-Larsen became a symbol of the Shetland Bus's contributions. He came to represent all of them. This is something of a paradox as he had ordinarily attempted to avoid the public eye.

Landing agents who were to establish radio stations along the Norwegian coast - one of the most important activities of the Shetland Bus. Here can be seen Perry Ørstenvik (on left) and Nils Roberstad eating a meal at the camp at Furefjellet in Bømlo in the spring of 1944.

to make contact with resistance organisations and groups, supply them with weapons and equipment, and provide them with instructions and training. If possible, they would also return with refugees. It was the British organisation for special assignments in occupied Europe, the Special Operations Executive (SOE), and the intelligence organisation Secret Intelligence Service (SIS), that were responsible for this traffic. In this manner, the military phase of the North Sea Traffic began.

The Shetland Bus did not have much to defend themselves with during the years the traffic between Norway and Shetland took place in fishing boats.

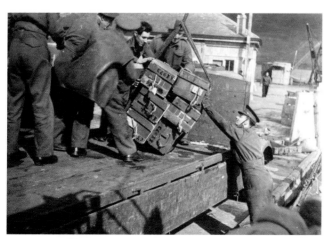

Military equipment for the home forces in Norway is loaded in the harbour in Scalloway.

R.N.N.S.U.
SCALLOWAY
BASE

SHETLAND

The emblem of the Shetland base as it looked at the end of the war. The abbreviation stands for "Royal Norwegian Naval Special Unit".

Lerwick – the county town of Shetland – was often the refugees' first encounter with the free world. The picture shows Lerwick harbour just prior to the outbreak of war.

Lerwick

The first base of operations for the military traffic was established in Lerwick, the county town of Shetland, in the autumn of 1940. The first expedition landed in an area north of Bergen during Christmas, and by June 1941, when the sailing season ended, the «Shetland Bus» had completed 16 missions over the North Sea. Fishing boats had become naval vessels, and the fishers and sailors, soldiers. But they had little to defend themselves with. On the first missions they had only hand weapons, and although the cutters were eventually equipped with machine guns on their decks, their defences were meagre against attack from German aircraft and patrol boats.

These activities required the utmost secrecy, and naturally could not take place in the lighter times of the year when chances of discovery by enemy aircraft and patrol boats were greater. If agents were unfortunate enough that their boat was detected, the Germans or their collaborators might still not realize their true errand, and mistake them for fishers. The registration number of the boat was therefore replaced with the registration number of a boat from the destined area so that the agents could remain as inconspicuous as possible.

Lunna Voe

It soon became clear that a relatively large town like Lerwick was not suitable as a base for an enterprise highly dependent on secrecy. It was therefore decided to move the base to a more peripheral location, one that could at the same time fulfil the other needs of the base. After deliberation, the choice fell on Lunna Voe (voe is the Shetland word for bay), about 50 kilometres north of Lerwick. The summer of 1941 was used to move from Lerwick to Lunna, where the operational crew was lodged in Lunna House, a 17th century manor. At this point it had also become clear that it was a security risk for SOE and SIS to share a common base; as a result, that summer SIS established its own base in Peterhead on the east coast of Scotland.

Besides the fact that the crews of the Shetland Bus found the isolated area around Lunna monotonous, the base was deemed satisfactory. It was possible to carry out activities without too much outside scrutiny; it was, after all, an extensive operation, with a great deal of traffic and tons of equipment being loaded onto the boats. Furthermore, the area was dotted with small stone houses in a variety of forms, well-suited for storing military equipment. The base functioned smoothly, with the exception of the men's discontent. Over 40 missions were sent forth from the base at Lunna to the Norwegian coast.

Scalloway

Eventually also Lunna's disadvantages became apparent. In particular, its location became inconvenient over time. Most supplies and equip-ment had to be acquired in Lerwick, where the boats also had to be transported for repairs. When a high-ranking British officer from London pointed out on a visit that the east-oriented base was exposed to attack, it became clear that a new location once more had to be found. This time the choice fell on Scalloway,

*Scalloway.
The slipway the
Shetland Bus had
built can be seen
in the middle of the
picture.*

a village on the west side of the island that boasted a boatyard, a significant advantage. Subsequently, there was another move and the preparation of a new base this summer too. Moreover, the Shetland Bus was placed under Norwegian command.

At the start of the sailing season in the autumn of 1942, the new base at Scalloway was ready, and the suitability of the new location quickly became evident. The crews, now numbering around 100 men, were much more content here than they had been at Lunna, and the workshop in the vicinity made maintenance much easier. Workshop owner Jack Moore put all his workers and equipment at the disposal of the base. The addition of a slipway was a further improvement, as boats could now be lifted out of the water for repair. The slip, Prince Olav Slipway, was a significant advance, and was inaugurated with much ceremony in October 1942.

Discovery and reprisals

Yet while conditions improved in Shetland, the severity of German counter-tactics intensified. Extensive use of informers and infiltrators led to crucial losses for the Shetland Bus. Worst hit was

The worst reprisals. Telavåg is obliterated.

Telavåg in April 1942. Here an infiltrator had exposed two agents from England, and in the Gestapo action that followed two high ranking Gestapo officers were killed. The Germans wreaked a gruesome revenge. Telavåg was levelled to the ground, and the entire population arrested. The men were sent to German concentration camps where 31 perished, while women, children, and men over 60 were interned for two years in Hardanger. One of the English agents was killed in action and the other executed, as was one of the Telavåg contacts. In Trandum another 18 men were shot as punishment. They had attempted to escape to England via Ålesund, but were exposed by Rinnan's agents who had presented themselves as fellow refugees. In the course of 1942, virtually the entire export operation was dismantled by the Germans. Furthermore, the Shetland Bus lost seven boats, with 33 men in all, primarily through shipwreck or German attack. It would have been tantamount to recklessness to continue the traffic.

Hessa, Hitra, and Vigra

Salvation arrived in the form of three new submarine chasers from the United States, christened *Hessa*, *Hitra*, and *Vigra*. The skippers were, respectively, Petter Salen, Ingvald Eidsheim, and the legendary Leif Andreas Larsen, a.k.a. «Shetlands-Larsen». All three already had considerable experience with

Sub-chaser Hessa photraphed at Leirvik in Stord in 1945.

Officers and crew on the Hessa.

the North Sea Traffic. «Sub-chasers» were a different breed from the cutters. While the latter could reach a maximum speed of around 5 knots, the sub-chasers could attain 16 knots. Furthermore, the sub-chasers were much better armed, including cannons at both the stern and the bow and a Colt machine gun on each bridge wing. According to the Shetland base, between November 1943 and war's end the sub-chasers completed altogether 120 missions between Norway and Shetland. One hundred agents were landed on the Norwegian coast and two hundred agents and refugees carried back to Shetland. After the three sub-chasers were put into operation, the Shetland Bus did not lose a singe man or vessel. Altogether, the Shetland Bus transported 192 agents and 383 tons of military equipment to the Norwegian coast during the war, returning with 73 agents and 373 refugees. While the England Crossing was primarily a western Norway phenomenon, the Shetland Bus's activities stretched over a much greater geographical area. For example, a series of tours went to the Trøndelag districts and to Nordland.

Inestimable importance

Was the North Sea Traffic significant for the progression and outcome of World War II? This question is too com-prehensive to be satisfactorily dealt with here. Yet what we can affirm is that the North Sea operations played a pivotal role in the recruitment of soldiers for the foreign-based Norwegian forces. Most of these were assigned to the navy and the merchant marine, priorities of the Allies due to the critical importance of maintaining supply lines to Great Britain, and later to the Soviet Union. We know that

The home forces in action in Bergen during the liberation in 1945, with Sten Guns and other equipment brought over by the Shetland Bus during the war years.

Norwegian seamen, civilian and military, made a central contribution to this work. Here must also be mentioned all the wireless operators landed by the Shetland Bus along the Norwegian coast in order to inform the Allies about German ship movements in the northern arena. Also this was crucial for the maintenance of supply lines.

Furthermore, we can without hesitation assert that the achievements of the Shetland Bus were of inestimable importance to the construction of a nation-wide resistance movement in Norway. It is difficult to conceive of any other way in which the movement could have been supplied what it needed in the way of instructors and military material. Moreover, that the military resistance, especially in the final phases of the war, contributed to engaging large numbers of German troops in Norway that could otherwise have been active on other battlefronts, there can be no doubt. When the transition from war to peace went so smoothly in May 1945, it was the military resistance movement *(Milorg)* that held most of the honour.

The link over the North Sea to Great Britain was also of vital importance on the moral and psychological levels. The knowledge that one could carry on the fight against tyranny from the other side of the North Sea, and the awareness that there was a path over the sea to a place of freedom for the persecuted, set off a veritable «England fever» along major sections of coastal Norway. On Norway's west coast it spread like fire in dry grass, resulting in the departure of thousands. For those who remained to take up the fight inside the nation's borders, the connection over the North Sea was a powerful catalyst for the maintenance of morale and the will to fight. And when the boats came ashore with agents, weapons, and other military equipment, «England fever» was hardly less among those who had stayed than with those who had left. There can be no doubt that when relations between Great Britain and Norway were better at the end of the war than they ever had been, this can be credited to the North Sea Traffic.

Several refugees found spouses on the other side of the North Sea. Barbara Christie from Scalloway and Arne Olsen Melkevik from Telavåg were married in January 1944. Here photographed with their best man Birger Igland from Bremanger and maid-of-honour Rosaleen Sinclair from Scalloway. Note the small Norwegian flag on Barbara's wedding dress.

Arild Rypdal *(b.1934) is one of Norway's foremost suspense writers – often described as a modern crime writer of international stature. Since his debut in 1991, the erstwhile pilot, engineer, and airport director has published a novel every year. Rypdal's books deal with global politics, with a special emphasis on the British intelligence organisations MI-5 and MI-6. In 1992 he received the Riverton Prize, «The Golden Revolver», for best crime novel.*

The inspiration for Rypdal's political thrillers originates in his wartime experiences when, seven years old, he fled to England with his family. There, through his father's secretive job, he had his first encounter with the British intelligence service. Rypdal's writing is often a blend of fiction and reality, but he claims that his books are not about his family.

We have invited Arild Rypdal to write the beginning of the book he never wrote – the book about himself. The story of how he became a suspense writer.

The flight

I was seven and four months and my younger brother was three and a half. We were living in a modest house completed the year before, four miles from the centre of Ålesund. Although Ålesund was a fishing town, my father was a businessman.

The German occupation lay like a blanket of darkness over everything. People whispered, food was scarce, travel and radios were forbidden. In the schools, we now learned German instead of English.

The winter of 1941-42 was particularly harsh. Non-stop gales thrashed the six-foot high snow into huge drifts. There were comings and goings after dark in our home, with no explanation for us children; my father regularly swept

away footprints in the snow. There were other mysterious things, too. Our meagre rations were occasionally supplemented with British military field supplies. American coffee appeared from nowhere, replacing the hated ersatz type. In a box buried in the snow in our garden, I found a radio transmitter. My mother told me it was a device for scaring off mice. Our mantelpiece was full of pictures of a strange man. A few days later, a picture of the same man appeared in the paper. «Shot dead in the street,» read the caption.

The perpetrators had escaped. The mysteries multiplied. For a small boy, it was a time of thrills and frights in an eerie silence. Questions were as dangerous as answers.

Then came the day when my mother fetched me out of school in the middle of class. She was in a great hurry and told the teacher that we were going fishing. Even I did not believe that, since the weather was terrible. Luckily, the teacher was of the right sort. He told no one.

She had packed one suitcase, but that was not nearly enough. My brother and I had to don several layers of clothing. I didn't know at the time, but my father could not come near our home, nor could any of the members of his resistance group, Antrum. We had to make our own way to Ålesund to rendezvous with him. The Germans had seized all cars and there was no petrol to be had. Taxis were few and far between; miraculously, one came to pick us up. A big wood-fired gas generator on the rear fender helped it cough slowly along.

Ålesund was in a state of siege. The Germans had cordoned off everything, and patrols were everywhere. Both my mother and the driver were terrified that our suitcase would be noticed. It was a giveaway.

In town we met my father in a dark warehouse. In Ålesund water is everywhere, with two canals running through it and the sea on three sides. My father had arranged for a small boat to take us over to the island of Vigra. The waters around Ålesund were being patrolled by German «E-boats» in tight chain formations; they stopped and inspected all boats. Ours was so small that it could appear to be an open, one-man craft. In the bow was a pitifully small covered cabin. We all squeezed in there, my father insisting on silence. The owner of the boat stood at the stern, steering by tiller. To anyone familiar with things nautical, it would have been obvious that the little boat was bow-heavy and that something was concealed there; but the sentries on the E-boats did not catch on, though they studied us through binoculars. We made it through without event.

Once on Vigra, we were faced with a five-mile march through heavy snow. A freezing gale beat at us all the way up to the house of a friend of my father's – one Petter Molnes. What we did not know was that the Gestapo were in the midst of a raid, going from door to door waving machine guns, kicking in doors and screaming orders. Unwittingly, we had passed through to the wrong side of the cordon. Petter's wife said he was not at home, but he came out from behind the door when he heard it was us. He explained that it was impossible for us to stay there because he was expecting the Gestapo at any moment. We had to make our way back to the south end of the island, where the Gestapo had finished for the time being. Thinking back, it was almost madness. A family of complete strangers with one suitcase on an island that had served as a way station for the majority of the illegal traffic across the sea.

We were on the point of collapse, when we were hospitably taken into the family Blindheimsvik's home on the south shore of the island. It was an extremely courageous thing for them to do. We would have been impossible to explain, since my father was a well-known and wanted resistance leader. We stayed for two days, maintaining total silence. My baby brother was not even allowed to cry, and was immediately wrapped in blankets if he did.

I knew nothing of it at the time, but the Antrum's radio operator had very bravely gone on the air in the midst of the alarm. In manually punched out Morse code, he informed London of the calamity in Ålesund and that all of Antrum were attempting to escape the consequences of an infiltration by the traitorous Rinnan Band. London alerted the so-called Shetland Bus, which operated the illegal route across the North Sea. In their turn they signalled a boat they had on stand-by west of the minuscule and uninhabited island of Erkna. The boat was *Heland*, and the skipper was Sevrin Roald, himself from Vigra. All this took time of course, with the necessary encryption and manual transmission for each link, and then the rendezvous information had to follow the same route back.

The second night we were suddenly called

out. Standing on a small jetty in pitch darkness and a howling wind, we waited silently. After a while we heard the soft dunk-dunk-dunk of a Norwegian single-cylinder semi-diesel at tickover speed. These big engines rotated so slowly you could easily count their strokes.

In an unbelievable feat of navigation, the boat was suddenly there alongside the jetty. At the time, radar and echo-sounders did not yet exist. Sevrin Roald must have found his way by the smell of home, said my father later.

Everything happened in a matter of seconds. People swarmed out from their hiding places: from under the jetty, from behind the boathouse, from snowdrifts. I was stiff with fear, thinking it was a German ambush, but then I understood. People were piling over the gunwale and disappearing below deck. They filled the crew's cabin in the forepeak as well as the hold. Since there were children in our family, we got the skipper's cabin behind the engine, right over the propeller. The dunk-dunk changed to a donk-donk-donk as the skipper reversed the propeller. The boat had been at the jetty for a scant 30 seconds, then it slid back into the darkness.

Normally, the crossing should have taken eighteen hours, but the storm increased to an unbelievable blizzard against which we made very slow progress. The voyage took two days and three nights. We were all immediately and violently seasick, and all I can remember of those terrible days was the little cabin floor awash with vomit. Every now and again the boat would list so much that we thought it was capsizing, rolling us off our bunks and into the slime. I can also remember one especially terrible moment: On the second day, my father struggled up the ladder to have a look at the weather. He stood for five seconds in the open hatch, and came down a changed man. His face had gone grey. Wordless, he sat on the edge of the bunk and buried his

face in his hands. My mother prayed. Obviously, they didn't think the little craft could ride out that ferocious storm.

On the third morning, everything was suddenly very quiet. The only sound was the rhythmic throbbing of the engine, with a new note of vigour. It went tottotonk-tottotonk at full speed. We all hurried up to the deck. Staring open-mouthed at the unfamiliar landscape of rolling hills, I saw that we were entering a bay, and that there were a large number of Norwegian fishing boats riding their moorings in the centre of the bay.

«Guess where we are,» said my mother in a voice happier and clearer than I had heard it since before the war.

«England!» I answered, without hesitation. Close enough. It was Lunna Voe in the North of Shetland.

Arild Rypdal

Escape

«I leave tonight for
England»

The England Quay

A narrow mountain shelf.
A rusty bollard.
Like natural monuments
they recount the flight to England,
the boats that waited,
the people who longed.

The traffic from the tiny settlement was so great
the island shelf west in the sea was dubbed the England quay.

Hernar in Øygarden, Hordaland

Name: Karsten Severin Danielsen
Born: 04.05.1925
Place of birth: Andvik in Masfjorden, Hordaland
Residence: Fjøsanger in Bergen, Hordaland

Left his family in Askøy for Shetland at only 16 years of age.

«Dear Mum and Dad - I leave tonight for England»

Hearing about neighbours and friends who had crossed the North sea was exciting. «England fever» was contagious, and it spread rapidly among the youth of western Norway. Instead of hanging around home watching the Germans, one should instead escape to England and join the Allies. Many caught «England fever», among them 16-year-old Karsten Danielsen and his friends on Askøy. It had been the topic of their regular Sunday gatherings. They became more and more determined to cross over.

– We thought living in an occupied country was dreadful. We ached to be rid of the Germans, says Karsten, back on the same pier he departed from.

They first went to look over a boat they had decided to «acquire», but the owner of the boat had been wary and had removed part of the motor. The choice then fell on *Gullborg*, a 56-foot fishing boat, auspiciously located. Just before they cast the hawser that September evening in 1941, three boys came bicycling full speed towards the boat. They

wanted to join them to England. The escape was no more secret than this. The news had spread. When they finally set their course due west, 26 people were on board.

– If anyone had said anything to my parents, I wouldn't have made it. They would have locked me in a room. The young runaway, a secondary school student, did not dare reveal his plans to his parents. He left them a letter instead:

«Dear Mum and Dad and everyone else. I leave tonight for England. We have arranged everything in advance so we need only shove off. If you find this letter tonight, you mustn't say anything before tomorrow morning. By then we will be far away. I have taken some personal things and clothes with me. It won't be long before we return. Some others from Davanger are joining us. Much love, Karsten."

But helping to save his country didn't turn out to be as glamorous as the young man had hoped. First he was offered a clerical position in London, but the battle-hungry sixteen-year-old hadn't fled his land only to sit in an office. In the end, he found work in the merchant marine. On a run-down tanker he worked in the mess, responsible for washing dishes. This is how exciting fighting for your land could be.

– Life on the ship was difficult and bleak. I cried myself to sleep several nights. At those moments I regretted ever having left home.

Name: Ivar Birger Refsnes
Born: 26.12.1921
Place of Birth: Ålesund, Møre and Romsdal
Residence: Ålesund, Møre and Romsdal

Crossed the North Sea in one of the smallest boats used in the England Crossing.

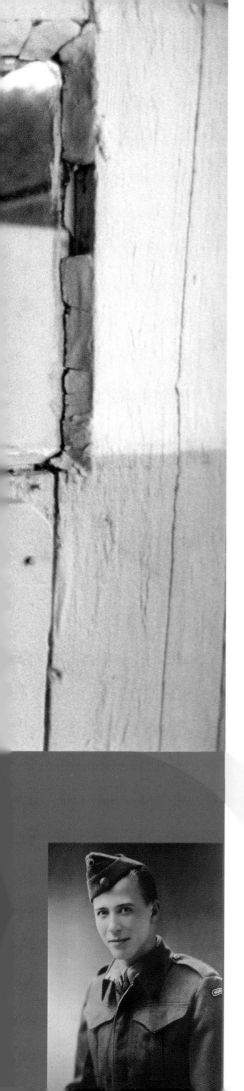

«Finding Shetland was pure luck»

— I would never have done it again, says Ivar Refsnes of Ålesund, back in the half-open motorboat *Klegg* sixty years after the war. The 22-foot boat is on display in a museum, evidence that people used every kind of craft they could get their hands on in their attempts to cross the North Sea.

In the stern of the fishing boat is a small wheelhouse, and in the bow a little cabin which could seat three people. The wheelhouse only has space for one person. This meant that the seven youths would have had to take turns sitting out on the deck during the four days it took to get to Shetland.

— It was insanity. None of us had navigated by map and compass before. We were landlubbers. Not even the owner of the boat had been far enough out to sea to lose sight of land. We had simply no idea what we were about, recounts Ivar Refsnes, who still doesn't know how they managed to find Shetland.

He was twenty years old, just finished with business school, when in August 1941 he heard about two fellows who were looking for people to join them in crossing the North Sea. Together with three school friends, he «signed up». The boat was now full.

— At home I told them I was going to help someone out with some work and wouldn't be back that night.

The parents and five brothers he left behind soon understood where he was. Many young people from Ålesund departed in the same manner that year.

«My boyfriend lured
me to an unfamiliar
country»

Escaped to Shetland with her boyfriend.

Name: Klara Signe Nybø
Maiden name: Værøyvik
Born: 24.03.1920
Place of birth: Jølster, Sogn and Fjordane
Residence: Værlandet in Askvoll, Sogn and Fjordane

Student Klara Værøyvik (married name Nybø) was home on summer vacation when she found out that her boyfriend, Per Johan, was planning to leave for Shetland. Twenty-one-year-old Klara still had one year left at the teaching institute in Levanger, but the fisherman who had stolen her heart now lured her to an unfamiliar country.

– I was the oldest of seven children, and my father was a widower. I felt I couldn't shirk my family responsibilities, says the now-aging coastal dweller. She deliberated for several days before finally saying yes, joining her boyfriend, her two-years-younger brother Trygve, and 16 other refugees.

Women couldn't be soldiers. That was the assumption during the Second World War. As a result, few women crossed the North Sea to enlist themselves in the services. This Klara knew. «But there must be something I can do?» thought the love-struck young woman. So she hopped on board the fishing boat with her boyfriend.

Back on the pier stood her 45-year-old father. For several days he had been trying to convince her not to leave, but one August evening in 1941 the fishing boat *Solveig* «tocked» away with his two oldest children. Trygve never returned.

Klara still lives on the island Værlandet in outer Sunnfjord. It was this fishing settlement her boyfriend lured her away from, but it was also here they returned to settle down after marrying in Scotland during the war.

Klara remembers well the night she left. Their departure was supposed to be secret, but when the boat set sail many people were waving from

the pier, among them a 78-year-old grandfather who was saying good-bye to the last two boys from his home. The young woman stood in the wheelroom so she could see the 460-metre high mountain on the neighbouring island of Alden as long as possible. By the time the landmark faded into the horizon, her seasickness had become so severe that she regretted the entire trip.

– What have I got myself into? What will I do in a strange country? wondered the student teacher where she lay on sacks of straw in the *Solveig's* hold.

After more than a day's sail they arrived in Shetland, but the journey was far from over. Accompanied by a military guard from Shetland, they were sent on an equally long sea voyage to Buckie in northern Scotland. The trip continued to Aberdeen, where trains awaited, «Refugees from Norway» chalked in large block letters on the sides of the cars. Women and men were separated, and Klara had to bid farewell to her boyfriend. In London, they were interned and interrogated in an attempt to flush out spies. Twelve days later, in September 1941, she stood in the middle of Piccadilly Circus, her British registration card in her hands. It had been a long trip from the little fishing community to world metropolis London.

Everyone had to do something for their country. Even women who couldn't be soldiers. There was no alternative. Klara knew this. She registered as a nurse, but was asked if she would help to start a Norwegian school in Scotland. She accepted. Teaching student Klara Værøyvik served as a teacher in a three-hundred-year-old castle just south of Aberdeen.

Name: Kirsten Landøy
Maiden name: Værøy
Born: 11.06.1916
Place of birth: Værlandet in Askvoll, Sogn and Fjordane
Residence: Værlandet in Askvoll, Sogn and Fjordane

Name: Greta Landøy
Maiden name: Landøy
Born: 10.05.1942
Place of birth: Glasgow, Scotland
Residence: Værlandet in Askvoll, Sogn and Fjordane

Name: Anton Johannes Landøy
Born: 09.11.1918
Place of birth: Værlandet in Askvoll, Sogn and Fjordane
Residence: Værlandet in Askvoll, Sogn and Fjordane

The young couple fled from Værlandet, but found life in a foreign land more difficult than at home.

«We fled
to the war»

The newly-married couple fled occupied Norway for fear of being ordered to work for the Germans. Yet this did not mean life became easier for 22-year-old Anton Johannes Landøy and 25-year-old Kirsten Landøy after they set off in a fishing boat from the little island community of Værlandet, furthest out in Sunnfjord.

He was called into the nerve-wracking convoy traffic over the Atlantic in which more than two thousand Norwegian sailors lost their lives. She remained behind alone, with a newborn daughter in a foreign land.

Burned into his memory is the scene that occurred every time Anton Johannes set out to sea again after a few days' leave with his family in Scotland. The young father held his daughter in his arms right up to the very moment he had to return her to her mother and board the train. She would cry and scream, «Papa, Papa! You mustn't leave us!». Neither could Kirsten hold back the tears. She knew too well that seamen were torpedoed in the Atlantic every single day. Alongside Anton Johannes stood other fathers listening to the same entreaties not to leave.

– Rows of mothers and children stood crying in English and Norwegian. It was a horrible strain, remembers Kirsten, who refused to travel by train for years after the war. The memories of an arduous time in a foreign country were too strong.

The young pair soon realised that they had not fled from the war but rather to it. Home in Værlandet life went on as usual; people there were for the most part unaffected by the war. On the other side of the North Sea they lived in fear for their life almost every day. He slept with a life vest for a pillow, continually fearing a submarine attack; she regularly ran to bomb shelters with her little girl.

– I missed home terribly, says Kirsten about her time in Glasgow and Newcastle. She went often to the beach to bathe in the same sea that washed up against the shore in Værlandet. This helped her feel closer to those at home.

The little family did everything they could to be together. Yet this wasn't so easy with Anton Johannes gone for months on tours to and from the USA. He just managed to be present at Greta's birth in Glasgow, but had to leave again the same day.

– Little Greta saved my life, says Anton quietly. He explains that his desire to be home with his family became so powerful that he transferred to the coast guard just before Christmas of 1942. The boat he had sailed on for over a year was torpedoed on its next tour. All 35 on board were killed.

The young couple on Værlandet have grown old. They have brought seven children into the world. Little Greta has her own grown children, and lives only a stone's throw from her parents.

– We'll never forget our years on the other side of the North Sea, but it's here we belong, they say, gazing out over the sea.

Name: Einar Jacob Kvalsvik
Born: 20.03.1921
Place of birth: Kvalsvik in Herøy, Møre and Romsdal
Residence: Fosnavåg in Herøy, Møre and Romsdal

Felt pressured to do as all the others
– cross the North Sea.

Nineteen-year-old Einar Kvalsvik felt the pressure from adult neighbours. «Haven't you gone over yet?», asked the men on the island furthest out in Søre Sunnmøre. It was like you weren't a man until you had crossed over the North Sea.

News of the departure of one boat after another spread quickly in the community, which didn't make things any easier. «So you're still messing about here?» the fathers and other adults would comment.

– In a way, you were ridiculed for not being man enough to get yourself over.

For the fisherman and seaman from Kvalsvik, just outside Fosnavåg, it wasn't for a lack of wanting to leave. He had been forced into German service and had crewed a German cargo ship along the coast. He detested working for the Germans, and had more than once tried to find his way over to England. But something had always foiled his plans.

His first escape attempt was immediately after the capitulation in the spring of 1940. He had just returned from the seal hunt, and an old coal boat was made ready to head westward. The boat was cut off by the Germans before it got that far. The next attempt was while he was in German service in Trøndelag in 1941. Together with a friend, he tried to cross the Tydal mountain range over to Sweden, yet had to abandon the attempt due to severe weather.

His restlessness was not lessened after he returned home and heard about everyone who had already crossed the North Sea .

– I knew many of those who'd left, and people talked incessantly about England – especially young people.

For their next escape they tried a fishing boat in the harbour, but had to give this up when a rumour went around that the Germans were up to something in Ålesund. Not long after this they made yet another attempt, this time with an old pilot boat, but two German patrol boats suddenly appeared in the harbour. Again the escape plans were scuttled. It wasn't until two and a half years later that Einar managed to get over. Together with four other fishermen from Kvalsvik he took the 47-foot fishing boat *Signal*, arriving in Shetland in mid-July 1944. This was his fifth attempt.

«You weren't a man until you left»

Name: Frank Mohn
Born: 29.04.1916
Place of birth: Nesttun in Bergen, Hordaland
Residence: Kråkenes in Bergen, Hordaland

Fled to England to join the English invasion of Norway.

– I left in order to join the invasion of Norway. We intended to return on the next boat, armed and ready. This is why we left – not to stay there for three to four years accomplishing nothing.

Frank Mohn, the Bergenser who after the war gained renown as a successful businessman, was one of many battle-hungry young men who crossed over the North Sea early in the war. He wanted to return with the Englishmen to throw out the Germans.

The twenty-five-year-old businessman had himself taken part in the battles on Valdres, and after the capitulation he continued the fight independently. Together with a group of friends, he gathered weapons that had been hidden in Voss. The group wanted to be ready to assist the English soldiers when they arrived.

– We felt something had to be done. We stockpiled weapons and plotted organised resistance. We were expecting an invasion – that the English would come over.

When the British invasion was slow to materialise, in September 1941 Frank crossed over to England, joined the Norwegian army, and prepared himself for the return to Norway. His disappointment was great when he discovered that the English were not planning to invade Norway.

– We couldn't comprehend that we weren't going back to fight, says Frank Mohn, remembering all the combat-ready young men who trained throughout the war in the Scottish mountains, yet never received an opportunity to exercise their skills.

A knee injury put a stop to the resister's military career. Instead, he was assigned responsibility for building a Norwegian slipway in Buckie in northern Scotland. The «Royal Norwegian Slipway and Repair Shop» was to take hand of the Norwegian fishing boats that had transported refugees across the North Sea. The businessman from Bergen restored boats for various types of military service.

His work in Buckie inspired Frank Mohn to continue in the same vein when he arrived home. Two generations after his industrial adventure in northern Scotland, the Bergen entrepreneur has built up an empire in the mechanical industry, boasting 1200 employees and eleven subsidiaries, both in and outside Norway.

– Without that knee injury, my future might have been very different. Then it might have been a military career instead of industrial enterprise for me, he concedes.

«I left in order
to return armed
and ready»

Name: Martin Peder Bjørlo
Born: 04.09.1921
Place of birth: Ålesund, Møre and Romsdal
Residence: Ålesund, Møre and Romsdal

Crossed the North Sea with the largest group to make the trip in one boat.

«I asked her to wait for me»

Martin Bjørlo was by no means forced to cross the North Sea. His incentive was a burning desire to take part in what was happening in England. Not that he knew so much about what was actually happening on the other side of the North Sea, but they were working to liberate Norway, weren't they? In this sense, twenty-year-old Martin was typical of the Norwegians who got themselves over to Shetland, freedom's western outpost, and from there further to England. They were young, single, and adventurous.

Almost since the arrival of the Germans, the office worker at Møller Motor in Ålesund had been attempting to find a boat heading to Shetland. In November 1941 he succeeded. One of his colleagues was going to make the journey.

– Can you get me a place? asked Martin. The next day came the answer. He had been accepted.

Sixty years later he is again on the peninsula below Borgund Church. It was here he left from. Here he stood in his winter coat and everyday hat. In one pocket he had two slices of bread. In the other was an extra pair of socks. Suitcases, sacks, and sportswear, all of which could attract attention, were forbidden.

The trip had been meticulously planned by an export group in Ålesund. Martin and two others had been told to meet up at Miss Sanne's at 5 pm. There they received instructions to make their way to Borgundgavlen where they would be contacted by others. Soon there were almost 25 people hiding near the shoreline. From here the group boarded a motorboat with a large cargo of corn in tow. Better camouflage could not be had for the trip to Ulsteinvik, where the 73-foot iron boat *Erkna* waited. The same night the *Erkna* turned her bow westward with sixty refugees on board – the largest group taken over in one craft during the England Crossing.

No one knew that Martin was leaving for England. By chance, on the way to the boat he met Aase – a young woman he had been dating occasionally the last few months. She immediately surmised his destination, and he confirmed her suspicion. They exchanged a parting kiss before continuing on their ways. She promised to keep his secret.

– We made a pact to meet again when everything was over.
Six years later they were married.

«It started to burn under our feet»

The Remøy family regularly met boats from Shetland, and had more than once helped people who needed to escape the country. Towards the war's end they came into the Gestapo's searchlight themselves, and the family of seven with the fisherman father had to flee. Consequently, siblings Magnus, Gjertrud, and Bjarne Remøy became the last Norwegian refugees to cross the North Sea.

– We had been quite active, and finally the situation became too heated. It started to burn under our feet and we had to escape, say the three siblings from Remøy in Sunnmøre.

Six decades after the war, nothing about the ordinary wooden building on Remøy reveals what kind of activities the family had been involved in. Yet if the walls could speak, they would tell of secret agents anxiously awaiting boats from Shetland, of the refugee who left behind an expensive coat, and of the messengers who so often arrived with instructions telling where the next load of weapons should be picked up or delivered.

Unmarried siblings Magnus and Gjertrud have lived in the family house their entire lives, but they seldom speak of what happened then. Nor does their brother Bjarne, who lives in the neighbouring house, speak much more about this period. This is what they had been taught: they should know as little as possible, and they should speak as little as possible.

With some reluctance, Magnus and Bjarne describe the boats from Shetland, the weapons shipments they went along to pick up, the salt bin with the secret room, the hiding places out on the islands, and the people they hid. Gjertrud tells about the soap and coffee she received on board the Shetland «buses», as they were called, and about the stories she had to spin to cover for her father's activities.

At the end of April 1945, just before the end of the war, things almost went awry. A resistance member was apprehended in Ålesund, and the family on Remøy received a message that the Gestapo were on to them. They removed all traces and buried a bag of English coffee in the field. The men took off for the mountains and their mother left for an aunt's house. At home Gjertrud cleaned while her sister played their organ so it resounded throughout the community. Then the Gestapo came.

– The Gestapo came to the door and asked about our father. I said that he was in the districts, chopping wood, and that he would be gone a few days, remembers Gjertrud, who, amazingly enough, managed to remain perfectly calm.

The next day they moved the ammunition supplies to a safer place, gave away the cow and hens, packed warm clothing, and turned the key in the door. The entire family vanished – or went into hiding, as was said. Some days later they were on their way to Shetland on one of the Shetland buses they knew so well.

Gerhard, his wife Lovise, and their children Magnus, Georg, Bjarne, Lilly, and Gjertrud, arrived in Shetland as late as 3rd May, 1945. They were not only the last to cross over. They were also among the few who crossed back to Norway on the legendary Shetland Bus a few days before the Norwegian national day, 17th May.

Name: Gjertrud Remøy
Maiden name: Remøy
Born: 28.02.1918
Place of birth: Remøy in Herøy, Møre and Romsdal
Residence: Remøy in Herøy, Møre and Romsdal

Name: Bjarne Remøy
Born: 01.11.1926
Place of birth: Remøy in Herøy, Møre and Romsdal
Residence: Remøy in Herøy, Møre and Romsdal

Name: Magnus Remøy
Born: 12.11.1914
Place of birth: Remøy in Herøy, Møre and Romsdal
Residence: Remøy in Herøy, Møre and Romsdal

The family of fishers on Remøy were the last refugees to cross the North Sea.

«We helped many people
out of the country»

A Hiding Place near the Sea

With the sea as its nearest neighbour
the cowshed on Skorpa was an ideal hideaway.
Here lay everyman, and here lay Shetlands-Larsen.

They waited for a boat and they waited for the weather.
But most of all they waited for a message from London.
«The Shetland Bus arrives tonight.»

Skorpa in Herøy, Møre and Romsdal   *1*

«We helped many people escape»

Alfred Sortland was one of those who rendez-voused with refugees and helped hide them in barns and private homes. There they waited for boats that could carry them over the North Sea. He remembers especially one large group he sent off in February 1942.

Alfred hid the refugees' suitcases and backpacks in a tackle shed outside Svortland on Bømlo while they waited for *the Rupee*. This boat had been pur-chased by the resistance group in Bergen, while the escape had been coordinated by the Bremnes group.

Many of the approximately 40 refugees hiding on the island had managed to evade arrest when the Stein organisation was destroyed in Bergen. Now they were being pursued by the Germans and needed to flee the country. Like so many others in similar situations, they came to Bømlo, where a group had been established for the purpose of «exporting» refugees over the North Sea.

In the headlands in Strømsfjord, shop worker Alfred Sortland could breathe easier when the rhythmic knocking of the fishing boat's engine faded into the dark that winter day. The Bremnes group had helped another boatload of refugees escape to freedom. Little did Alfred know that the net was pulling in around him. This would be the last large group of refugees to cross the North Sea during the war.

Back at the hiding place the memories stream in. Alfred paid dearly for helping the refugees. Early in May 1943 life changed dramatically for the 24-year-old Bømlinger. His name had been beaten out of some poor fellow, and now the youth of Bømlo were to be punished for all the refugees who had escaped from the island. Alfred Sortland was to become NN-prisoner #6672, and would disappear in night and fog.

– It is impossible to describe what we went through. We had been sentenced to death and had no means of defence. We were to be eliminated. But first we were to work as long as there was life in us, remembers Alfred about the German concentration camps.

– One day my friend was so exhausted he sat down on a plank. They beat him to death. Hanging, shooting, and abuse were everyday fare for us. You could say we were wading in corpses.

Miraculously, Alfred survived the hell for a year and a half. But then began another battle - the fight to obtain assistance and to have his story believed. Physically, Alfred Sortland appeared to be completely healthy, but inside he was a destroyed man. More than twenty years passed before he could speak about what had happened. In 1998 he allowed his wife to write his memoirs, and he has since spoken to many school children about his experiences during the war.

Name: Alfred Sortland (used the name Gundersen during the war)
Born: 28.08.1919
Place of birth: Svortland on Bømlo, Hordaland
Residence: Svortland on Bømlo, Hordaland

Participated in exporting refugees to Shetland.

Name: Magnus Sigurd Hernar
Born: 18.06.1929
Place of birth: Hernar in Øygarden, Hordaland
Residence: Frekhaug in Meland, Hordaland

– Almost everyone out here helped the refugees. I remember we had two fellows from Osterøy staying in the south side of our attic for several weeks, and there were often people living in our smack, says Magnus Hernar.

Together with his cousin and friend Johannes Sture, he remembers well the busy war traffic home on Hernar. Boats came and went. More than a hundred people departed from the island, which at the time had 150 residents. The two curious fisherman's sons observed all the activity closely, and could not avoid noticing all the refugees hiding in barns and boathouses.

– We knew where they were going. England is just west of us.

It didn't take long before the young boys figured out that one of their neighbours was a chief organiser. One time they stumbled over a sizable weapons cache out on one of the uninhabited islands. This same neighbour came with the strict message that they must keep quiet about it – and they did. The boys, at that time at confirmation age, will never forget the day the Gestapo kicked in the door to their nearest neighbour. The German security police wanted the «exporter» who had helped so many refugees cross over to the British Isles. But they were too late. As for so many others, Hernar had been his last stop on his way out of the country.

Name:
Johannes Martin Sture
Born: 22.05.1926
Place of birth:
Sture in Øygarden,
Hordaland
Residence:
Hernar in Øygarden,
Hordaland

Inquisitive boys who lived on Hernar – the small fishing community that helped send so many refugees westwards.

During the war, Hernar, furthest out of Øygarden's islands, was a principal export point for refugees. People knew that here, on this island northwest of Bergen, there were Norwegians who could help them. Accordingly, small and large vessels from the entire district landed at the island to prepare themselves for the long journey over the North Sea, and strangers often arrived on the coastal shuttle from Bergen wondering if it was possible to make it over to England.

The auspicious location furthest west in the sea, together with the absence of German patrols, helps explain why the little fishing community held such a central place in the England Crossing. Yet the most important explanation is that here lived people who could hide refugees and organise their further transport.

«We knew where they
were going»

«I didn't want them to end up in the claws of the enemy»

Kristiane Stavland (married name Gilje) was a cook in Bergen when the war came, but she felt uncomfortable with all the German soldiers in the city, and in 1941 went home to Bømlo in Sunnhordland. Here she quickly became involved in efforts to smuggle people out of the country.

The cook in her mid-twenties did not operate through a resistance organisation. She hardly knew there existed people who were organising escape routes to the British Isles, and she had no idea that her community was one of the busiest export points in all of western Norway. It was by pure coincidence that Kristiane became involved.

– Irene, a cousin in Bergen, called with the message that there were some refugees on their way down on the coastal ship. She asked if I could meet them and help them in whatever way I could.

Kristiane did as her cousin asked. She met up on the pier dressed in a light-coloured top and a red knit jacket as agreed. A group of strangers accompanied her home to the family farm on Stavland, where they were to hide until they could get on a boat heading west. This is how

Kristiane came to aid four desperate refugees who had to escape when the Stein-organisation was exposed in Bergen.

~ No one was to see them, so they lived in our fishing boat which was moored below the house. Every night after dark I brought them home for supper. This went on for over a week.

Although Kristiane knew little about the organised resistance, she knew there was contact between the islands in west Norway and the free world on the other side of the North Sea. Five of her brothers had already headed in that direction, and she would herself soon discover how critical it was for the Germans to stifle that contact. The Stavland name had reached the ears of the Germans, and in 1942 both she and her brother were arrested. Kristiane was let off lightly with only a few months in prison, but her brother was deported to Germany.

With five brothers in England and one captured by the Germans, 27-year-old Kristiane was alone with her parents. Yet neither her own prison term nor the fact that the men on the farm were gone stopped the resister from Stavland. She had aided refugees before and she was ready to do it again.

– I didn't want them to end up in the claws of the enemy, and I believed it was the duty of a good Norwegian to help, she says outside her family home on Bømlo, where she more than once concealed refugees.

Name: Kristiane Gilje
Maiden name: Stavland
Born: 08.01.1915
Place of birth: Stavland on Bømlo, Hordaland
Residence: Urangsvåg on Bømlo, Hordaland

«We repaired boats that were used to cross over to England»

Name: *Arnt Kåre*
Fiskerstrand
Born: 16.06.1927
Place of birth:
Fiskarstrand in Sula,
Møre and Romsdal
Residence:
Fiskarstrand in Sula,
Møre and Romsdal

Helped repair
many boats that
were to cross the
North Sea.

From the little wharf on Fiskarstrand, just south of Ålesund, many boats made their way over the North Sea. They would often inexplicably vanish as soon as they were overhauled. Other times desperate refugees came to the home of the wharf owner looking for needed motor parts so they could make the trip the same night.

– It wasn't uncommon that as soon as we finished the boats and set them in the sea – they were turned towards England.

Arnt was a young apprentice in the family business «Fiskerstrand Wharf» when the war started. He was still in school, but worked just as much at the workshop his grandfather had established in 1909. Early in June 1941, he took part in oiling the hull of and then launching the fishing boat *Harald II*. The workers had barely arrived home before the boat set out from the pier with 17 refugees on board. Two days later it dropped anchor in Shetland.

The same thing had happened a few months earlier. Then it was the Nordnes that was in need of overhauling and repairs. One day the owner, Sverre Roald from Vigra, appeared with the following request: «Six men with death sentences are hiding in a cabin on the mountain. We have to get them over to England. Could you please finish the boat as quickly as possible?» The boat was ready in record speed, and as soon as it was launched it set off westwards.

Boat owners often removed the injector nozzle or other motor parts so that refugees couldn't take their boats. As a result, machine parts in the boats on the slipway were in high demand, and motor parts were often removed and used in other boats. Not infrequently this occurred with the aid of the wharf owners. This was not only common at Fiskarstrand, but at most workshops along the coast.

– I remember people would come in the middle of the night to get help starting a motor, or to get a motor part they needed in order to escape.

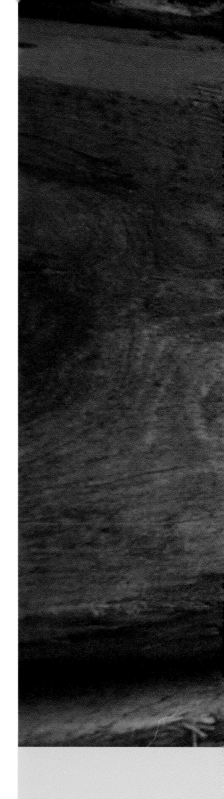

«We had refugees at our door all the time»

Name: Kari Robertstad Ringås
Maiden name: Robertstad
Born: 24.05.1929
Place of birth: Jelsa in Suldal, Rogaland
Residence: Stavanger, Rogaland

Night and day, refugees attempting to reach England came seeking refuge at the parsonage Kari called home.

– People often knocked on the door at night, remembers Kari Robertstad (married name Ringås) about the many refugees who frequented the parsonage she lived in on the island of Bømlo.

The youngest daughter of a priest was accustomed to strangers. Some lived in their house, while others laid low in the boathouse or with neighbours. Both Kari and her four-years-younger brother Per understood where the visitors were going. People on Bømlo spoke about Great Britain as if it was an island in the archipelago.

Her father, Pastor Peter Robertstad, was an important contact person who arranged for places for refugees to hide. In addition to hiding places at the parsonage in Finnås, he settled some with his brother, Nils, as well as with other neighbours. Nobody knows exactly how many refugees the priest helped, but on one night a group of forty people stood outside their door. Due to bad weather their boat had been forced to turn back, and it became the priest's job to conceal them. Other times Doctor Hus's car might swing up towards the parsonage with a family or two in need of shelter.

The pastor never refused to help. Nor did his wife Sofie, who prepared food and otherwise tended to the refugees as well she might. The adults did not try to conceal what was going on at home. Per

and Kari took part in most of the activities. Kari remembers that she had to stand watch when her father dug the radio out of the woodshed, and she had to run with her brother and down the well-beaten track when the Gestapo finally came and took her father.

– Many of the refugees were surprised that we accompanied our father, but he told them not to worry about us. We never said anything, says Kari outside the parsonage they moved away from in 1946.

Many of the faces will never fade for the parson's daughter. She will never forget the two kind boys who helped her with a school assignment just before they went on board the boat that was to carry them to Great Britain. But the name of the boat was *Blia*, and it disappeared in the waves. She also remembers the family that arrived in the middle of Christmas celebrations. The young girl was sad that strangers should come and ruin their Christmas. The parson did not share her feelings. For him it was more important to help people in need.

«Luckily it was me who found them and not the Germans»

Name: Lars Elier Mortensen
Born: 20.03.1915
Place of birth: Skudeneshavn on Karmøy, Rogaland
Residence: Skudeneshavn on Karmøy, Rogaland

Aided refugees who had been driven off course while attempting to reach Shetland.

Lars Mortensen was scouting for mackerel from the crow's nest on the mast of the *Sildøy*, when he spotted a boat drifting off the southern point of Karmøy.

– Trying to make it to England? asked the fisherman when he saw the little boat with four exhausted teenagers.

The youths from Bergen, a mere 16 to 19 years old, had planned to row to Shetland to enlist in the Norwegian forces. Instead they had ended up washing about in the sea for eight days in an open rowboat. Halfway to Shetland they had met a storm which had driven them back to Norway. Fatigued, soaked, hungry, and disoriented, they had felt certain they would never see dry land again. Yet the breeze and luck had had other ideas, propelling the open, four-oared boat into the fishing zone outside Karmøy. The provisions of tinned goods and the improvised sail on one oar left no doubt as to the youths' destination.

– You'll be fine boys. We'll lend you a hand, said the 26-year-old fisherman who, together with the rest of the crew of the *Sildøy*, was finishing the day's work

«If we hadn't been picked up by the fishers that day it would have been ugly. We were extremely tired, almost couldn't stand, and hadn't slept in several days. I doubt we could have handled much more because the wind picked up again soon after we came ashore,» wrote one of the four youths later in his journal.

The fishers hauled the refugees on board their fishing smack and tied the rowboat behind. Well in port, they concealed the boat and provisions under a lean-to.

– A friend came by and wondered what was going on. He was one-hundred percent Norwegian, but we didn't want anyone to know. My wife is from Askøy, so I said they were Judith's relatives who had come for a visit by boat.

The inquisitive neighbours having bought the story, the boys from Bergen could sleep peacefully in the smack. With «The Voice of London» on the radio, food in their stomachs, a bottle of gin to warm their bodies, dry clothes, and a decent roof, the boys couldn't have had it better. Before a breakfast of waffles, new-baked bread and milk had been laid out, Lars Mortensen had already arranged for his niece to take care of the weary sojourners. She had a cabin just outside of town where the boys could recover. A week later the four teenagers returned by the night boat to Bergen.

Shetland

«I picked up four Norwegian
refugees at the beach»

A Last Glimpse before Shetland

For the warriors from Shetland
the lighthouse was often the first they saw of Norway.
For those who were crossing to England, the white tower
and the green-clad rock were often their last glimpse of home.
Next stop Shetland.

Erkna in Giske, Møre and Romsdal

«I picked up four Norwegian refugees at the beach»

Name: Joan Mouat
Maiden name: Gray
Born: 10.01.1919
Place of birth: Norwick on Unst, Shetland
Residence: Norwick on Unst, Shetland

Met a Norwegian refugee family that landed near her home.

– We realised they had fled from the Germans and we offered them food and shelter. They were part of our family for two days, remembers Joan Mouat about the Norwegian refugee family she met on Unst – northernmost of the Shetland Isles.

When she encountered the Norwegian refugees, Joan was a newlywed living on the coast of Norwick with her husband, Andrew Duncan, his parents, a sister, and a brother. Their family shared a wall with a general store which they also managed, and the neighbours' sheep, cattle and two ponies grazed the land outside their home. When the boat refugees came ashore, they spied the lights of a pickup truck that Andrew Duncan was repairing near the beach. The weary family of refugees approached him. There was no need for them to explain where they were from. Nor did the British couple need to inform the family that they had reached their destination – the free world. Two days later they were ensconced in the Norwegian refugee camp in Lerwick, from where they would soon be heading to London.

Today, almost exactly sixty years later, Joan is now alone in the little building with its view of the beach. The store in the building beside them had to close in the 1970's after a ferry line had started up. The story of the Norwegian refugees is etched clearly in her memory.

The teachers from Espevær in Hordaland had refused to take part in a Nazi teachers' union, and had decided that it would be wisest to leave the country. On Easter evening 1942, together with four other refugees, Jan Hermann Hermansen, his wife Klara Helene (both teachers), and their children Jan Ottar and Solveig, set sail westwards on the fishing boat *Kapp*. The weather was poor and their motor stopped, but fortunately the storm drove them in the right direction – west. After five days they caught sight of land, and the teacher family went ahead in the lifeboat to see if they could make contact with anybody. Just before 11pm that night, the rowboat touched shore outside the Mouats' house. The next day the 25-meter fishing boat landed with the other refugees. It is hardly a coincidence that the family from Espevær landed at Unst – farthest north of the Shetland Isles. Closer to Norway they couldn't be. This is also the first island the Vikings reached when they came to Shetland in the 800's. Remains of Norwegian Viking farms, graves, boathouses, and the ruins of small churches can be found everywhere on the little island of barely 900

inhabitants. And like the rest of Shetland place names, the little village of Norwick still bears the name bestowed on it by the Vikings more than a thousand years ago.

– Norwegians were not foreign to us. I met many Norwegian and Swedish fishers here before the war. They came to the store to shop, recounts Joan in her peculiar dialect, so similar to the Norwegian language.

With the landing of Norwegian refugees on the same beach upon which the Vikings had disembarked a thousand years earlier, yet another friendship between the two lands was initiated. Since that time, Joan has steadily received enjoyable letters from Norway together with pictures of the refugee children who were then two and thirteen years of age. Furthermore, in case more Norwegians should come, Joan Mouat has gone to evening school to learn a little Norwegian.

«The boats arrived with refugees and Christmas trees»

James Wilbert Leask was barely ten years old when Norwegian refugees began to stream to his hometown – Lerwick on Shetland. The curious school boy was so fascinated by events in the harbour that he began to keep a journal. Today his notes have become suspenseful eyewitness accounts of a war.

«24th December 1944. Sunday evening the Norwegian torpedo boats (MTB's) 712 and 722 arrived. Half an hour later came a sub-chaser from the base in Scalloway, carrying refugees. 7th January 1945. More refugees, on the same sub-chaser. They look as if they've had a rough trip.»

It was the Norwegian torpedo boats (MTB's) that intrigued him most, and as a neighbour of the harbour he was regularly awoken by the din when they warmed up their engines in the morning. He counted the boats that left for missions to Norway, and he counted how many returned.

– They often came back with leaks and serious damage after battles in Norway. Then they pulled the boats right up on the slip, remembers James, who recognized the boats by their numbers.

From his classroom James had a view of the harbour, and he remembers well the sun-drenched October day in 1942 when the military boats arrived in Lerwick. It was the start of a diligently kept diary in a little blue notebook. He recorded his observations about the harbour almost every single day.

James also remembers the Norwegian refugees who came in on fishing boats early in the war. At that time the harbour was cordoned off with large barriers; nevertheless, the boy was able to observe what was happening. He saw German prisoners who had been picked up in the North Sea, and he saw boys his age disembark after rigorous sea journeys. Later he and his friends played on the small boats the refugees had had to abandon in the harbour. Yet most of all, he followed the activities of the Norwegian, British, Dutch, and Polish soldiers. He watched them play football and he saw them prepare cannons for their next mission. He saw boats return with dead and wounded, and he saw them arrive carrying refugees and Norwegian Christmas trees.

– Something happened every single day, re-members shop owner James Wilbert Leask, back at the harbour where the Norwegian language was commonly heard during the war.

Name: James Wilbert Leask
Born: 11.09.1930
Place of birth: Lerwick, Shetland
Residence: Lerwick, Shetland

Inquisitive youngster who kept a journal about events in Lerwick harbour.

Name: Elizabeth Anne Hoseason Morewood
Maiden name: Barclay
Born: 20.08.1930
Place of birth: Mid-Yell, Shetland
Residence: Mid-Yell, Shetland

Sheltered seven Norwegian refugees whose engine caught fire outside the island of Yell in Shetland.

Cold and wet, seven Norwegian refugees entered ten-year-old Elizabeth Barclay's (married name Morewood) front room in Shetland. After a protracted voyage over the North Sea, the motor of their fishing boat had caught fire near Yell – one of the northernmost islands of Shetland. As Elizabeth's parents possessed one of the largest houses in Mid-Yell, it became their responsibility to take charge of the refugees.

– The house was very busy. Mum tended an ugly knife cut on the hand of one of the men, while I was sent to fetch two relatives who could help make food, remembers Elizabeth. Like her brother, she had to give up her bedroom and move in with her mother and father.

Prior to this March day in 1941, the family on the quiet island had hardly noticed that the country was at war, but with seven refugees and two English soldiers in their house, the war came frighteningly near. Over the dinner table they heard how the boys in their early twenties had stolen the fishing boat *Ulabrand* in order to cross the North Sea. The boat had set out from Haramsøy north of Ålesund three days earlier, and had landed first at Unst. There they had taken aboard two soldiers, but on the way south they ran into motor problems outside Mid-Yell.

The island residents from one side of the North Sea listened eagerly to the island dwellers from the other side. The fishermen, store clerk, organ builder and electrician from Haramsøy described their lives at home. This was the first time Elizabeth had heard about Norway. She didn't understand much of the strange language, but one of them spoke a little English.

– They told us about snow and high mountains.

They also played such wonderful accordion music. This is how she remembers the refugees who, for two days, were part of her family.

One of the light-haired boys from Haramsøy taught her how to say «I love you». She has since learned much more, and now speaks fluent Norwegian. The encounter with the Norwegian refugees sparked off an intense interest in Norway.

Which is why Elizabeth Morewood reacted so strongly when, as an adult, she discovered a Norwegian grave that didn't have flowers on 17th May. All the other Norwegian graves had been decorated with flowers on the Norwegian national day. Now Elizabeth could read Norwegian and she soon dug up the story behind the nameless grave: only a few weeks before the refugees from Haramsøy came ashore in Yell, nine men from Haugesund had set off with the motorboat *Kantonella*. The boat never made it across, but after a terrible hurricane six bodies and some bits of wreckage washed up in Yell. Nobody knew who they were or where they had come from. The young bodies were buried as unknown Norwegians in the Mid-Yell cemetery where they shared a common gravestone.

Elizabeth had passed the anonymous grave on her way to church almost every Sunday. Yet not until 39 years after the wreck did the gravestone receive names, and the families home in Norway a grave to visit.

– I will never forget that day in 1980 when an entire planeload of Norwegian families came to visit the place were their boys lay, says Elizabeth Morewood outside the home where she met her first Norwegian refugees.

«They told us about snow and high mountains»

Name: Isabella «Bella»
Elizabeth Irvine
Maiden name: White
Born: 05.02.1929
Place of Birth: Lerwick, Shetland
Residence: Lerwick, Shetland

**Neighbour of the
Norwegian refugee
camp in Shetland.**

«We were told to stay away from Norwegians»

– Mum gave us strict orders to have nothing to do with Norwegians. They were scary foreigners, remembers Isabella "Bella" White (married name Irvine) about the war years.

The Norwegian refugee camp lay just below the eleven-year-old schoolgirl's home in Lerwick, Shetland. Large two-storey apartment buildings, in earlier times summer living quarters for herring girls at the herring station, were transformed into refugee camps for Norwegians while they waited to be sent on to interrogations in London. Many days might pass before the authorities managed to organize transportation; meanwhile, the refugees remained at the primitive camps on Browns Road. Only a hill and a fence separated the little girl from the foreigners from Norway.

– Mum was sceptical of foreigners. She didn't want us to have any contact with the Norwegians and subsequently forbid us to climb over the small wall that blocked a direct view of the refugee camp. But that made it all the more intriguing – so we climbed over anyway. This is how the inquisitive young girl met people from the other side of the North Sea.

Bella stood face-to-face with the first refugees when they walked up the steep hill just behind the house she shared with her mother and two younger sisters. She recalls especially well the two lovely girls in their twenties who had light, curly hair – not unlike her own. The Norwegian girls came all the way up to the metre-high wall separating the garden from the grass field beyond. The young women spoke with the little girl in Norwegian, also attempting sign language – without understanding each other. Yet the slightly uncertain smiles needed no translation.

She laughs about it all today as she stands in the little garden on Commercial Road.

– In many ways we lived an isolated life; we didn't know much about the world beyond the islands.

Now Bella is active in the «Shetland-Norwegian Friendship Society» and has many Norwegian friends. But at that time the world was different, and Norwegians were strangers.

«Would you marry
a seaman?»

Name: Albert Berg Eilertsen
Born: 10.07.1921
Place of birth: Gjøvik
on Senja, Troms
Residence: Lerwick, Shetland

Name: Davina Eilertsen
Maiden name: Pottinger
Born: 14.05.1921
Place of birth: Lerwick, Shetland
Residence: Lerwick, Shetland

Met in Shetland, married and settled down in Lerwick.

Many of the young men in Shetland had left for the war. Consequently, the young men from Norway were an enjoyable respite for the women who remained. Davina Pottinger was one of the local girls who met a Norwegian in uniform. Not long after, he asked her, «Would you marry a seaman?»

– He was so stylish in his uniform – and he spoke English so well, says Davina about the Norwegian man she met on Shetland.

– I had just come from the port and was bearded and dirty, but we agreed to meet at the dance the same evening, remembers Albert.

It was a rainy day around Christmas 1942 when the office girl from the local car mechanic's and the Norwegian navy sailor sought shelter under the same roof. No more was needed. Nine months later the two 21-year-olds from opposite sides of the North Sea were united in wedded bliss.

– We couldn't afford to get married in the church. We had a simple ceremony at the priest's home and afterwards held a reception with two or three friends in a borrowed room.

Sixty years later they again stand outside the town hall in Lerwick. It was here the dance they had agreed to meet at was held in 1942. It was to be a long dance. They have called the Shetland capital «home» for most of their time together since then, but they also lived for a period in Tromsø. It is for this reason the war bride with two passports speaks as much Norwegian as Shetland English, and the navy sailor who sailed with Shetlands-Larsen and the Norwegian MTB-boats during the war finds his words just as readily in English as in Norwegian.

The couple have always been there for each other – in good times and bad. Now they are weary. A hard life takes its toll. After the war she had to adjust to a life in which her husband was more at sea than at home. She had her job at the mechanic's and she had her daughter Synnøve (born in 1945). He couldn't manage to forget the war. His nerves finally went. At the age of 54, he retired.

Today Albert and Davina are living testaments to a time of strife that engendered lasting relations between two coastal peoples.

Shetland Bus

«We waged war from
fishing boats»

Secret Base

An inlet sheltered from the wind, a small wharf, an old manor
on a secluded bay:an ideal site for fishing boats secretly sent back to Norway.

Today only a small graveyard tells the tale of what took place here. A brass plate
on a wooden cross names a seaman who never came home.

Lunna, Shetland

«We would be returning to Norway»

Name: Otto Pletten
Born: 26.09.1920
Place of birth: Lygra in Lindås, Hordaland
Residence: Bergen, Hordaland

One of the first fishermen sent back to Norway on armed fishing boats, the popularly-called Shetland Bus.

Otto Pletten was first mate on the Bergen boat *Corvus* when war came to Norway. He signed off in Liverpool in order to enlist in the Norwegian military forces being built up in England and Scotland. There the 21-year-old from Lindås, just north of Bergen, was selected for special service by Martin Linge – the man whose name was synonymous with the specially trained soldiers in the Norwegian Linge company. Otto would return to Norway to operate behind enemy lines.

– We who were fishermen and seamen were chosen for the Shetland Bus. They didn't say much, but we understood that we would be sailing back and forth between Norway and Shetland. The sober retiree stands outside his white-painted house in Bergen, almost sixty years later to the day.

Otto was among the first fishermen who received military training before being sent to Shetland. Fishing and shipping had been his trades since he was knee-high, but shooting, sabotage, and the art of killing rapidly and effectively were new and challenging skills.

– We were to transport other Linge men who would carry out sabotage and establish radio bases in Norway. Our job was to shuttle them back and forth. We were to avoid battle situations, but we had weapons to defend ourselves with.

Otto speaks with a low voice when he recounts the tours to Norway. He says as little as possible. He mentions the failed action with the fishing boat *Nordsjøen*, which sank while they were laying out mines on the Norwegian coast. «The boat went down and we had to take another craft in order to get back to Shetland,» he says, without adding that they had had the Germans at their heels for five and a half days before managing to steal a boat and escape over the North Sea. Nor does he say anything about the friend and colleague who one minute was standing by his side, and the next had been torn overboard by a massive wave. Not one word is said about the fact that they drifted helplessly in the sea for four days while a hurricane pounded the little fishing boat *Arthur*. All this can be read in history books.

Otto Pletten is typical of these taciturn fishing boat warriors. Not even with his wife does he speak about the events of the war, while children seem less interested in such things. Yet one thing seems sad to him. That the names of many of the reticent warriors of the fishing boats were forgotten in all the fuss around Shetlands-Larsen after the war.

– Our names are supposed to be on the statue in the city, but I haven't been in to see it. All that is history now, says the man who stood shoulder-to-shoulder with Shetlands-Larsen on the precarious tours over the North Sea.

Name: Kåre Emil Iversen
Born: 10.10.1918
Place of birth: Flatanger in Namsos, North Trøndelag
Residence: Scalloway, Shetland

Joined the Shetland Bus and completed some fifty tours to Norway.

The first thing Kåre Iversen saw when he arrived at the special division in Shetland in October 1941 was a funeral. One of his thirty colleagues had returned lifeless from Norway. Barely 23 years old, Nils Nesse from Bømlo had been hit by enemy aircraft fire while returning to Shetland in a little fishing boat after having set an agent ashore.

The Shetland Bus's first loss was a grim reminder of the perilous job upon which Kåre was embarking.

All the same, nothing could deter the battle-hungry 23-year-old from Flatanger just outside Namsos. Two weeks after the funeral he began as a machinist on a fishing boat headed for Norway. Kåre Iversen was ready to do anything he could to throw out the Germans.

He is confused when asked how, hardly 23 years old, he could risk his life in that way. How could somebody ask such a ridiculous question? But he answers anyway.

– I wanted to inflict as much harm as possible on the Germans and quislings. They came into our land like thieves. That was my motivation.

The retired whale-fisher strolls along the Scalloway streets – the village that, for the most part, has been his home since the war. He had attempted to re-establish himself in Norway when the war ended, but found himself unable to settle in. In 1951, he returned his Norwegian passport.

The little village of one thousand housed the navy's special division during the last three years of the war. Now the streets are full of memories. He stops outside the large red building which has been dubbed the «Norway House». Here lived several of the crew. Across the street is a workshop and the slipway where the boats lay moored, awaiting orders to set sail for Norway. On the wall hangs a little sign reminding passers-by that Crown Prince Olav inaugurated the Norwegian slipway in 1942. Farther up the hill is the building that housed the local café – or canteen as the Shetlanders called it.

– On Sunday evenings we usually went to the café to talk to the local girls.

One Thursday in early December of 1944, he married Christina – one of the girls who worked at the café. But their honeymoon was brief. By Saturday he was at his post on the new sub-chaser *Vigra*, plying the waves towards Norway to pick up 19 refugees. But he returned – as always. The little village on the west side of Shetland had become his new home.

«I wanted to inflict
the greatest harm
possible on the
Germans»

Name: Olai Hillersøy
Born: 03.03.1915
Place of birth: Bulandet in Askvoll, Sogn and Fjordane
Residence: Bulandet in Askvoll, Sogn and Fjordane

Part of the special division that sailed to Norway on secret assignments.

– Think what we were to fight the war with. They were completely ordinary fishing boats mounted with machine guns, says Olai Hillersøy, shaking hid head.

Olai was one of the fishermen who went into the Shetland Bus. The experienced fisherman with a coastal skipper certificate and a rank of petty officer with the Norwegian navy was well acquainted with the fishing fields along the Norwegian coast. He quickly became a skipper on the militarised fishing boats. But the Germans caught on and poured considerable resources into stopping the camouflaged fishers. Olai Hillersøy remembers how exhausting it was to live in continual fear of capture.

– The smacks were hell. We used a day for each direction, and we only had a few small machine guns in some oil drums that we covered up with nets. But what good were they when we needed to defend ourselves against air attacks?

Long journeys and a sea full of mines. The skipper from Bulandet is convinced that it was the fishing boats that wore them down.

– The 15 to 20-meter-long smacks were difficult to manoeuvre. We knew we didn't have a prayer if we were attacked. We got used to having our hearts in our throats.

– Fortunately, we got a bottle of rum after every tour so we could relax. The first drink we had to blend. The rest went down straight.

In the spring of 1943, the military leadership realised that the fishing boats' time was over. In the course of the winter they had lost seven boats and more than thirty men. The 28-year-old fisherman from Bulandet had been lucky – with eleven or twelve tours over the North Sea behind him, in constant battle with aircraft and inclement weather, he was still alive.

– The sub-chasers were like going from hell to heaven. This is how he characterises the new military boats with the big cannons sent from the USA that same autumn. The three new boats sailed well-over one hundred missions to Norway without a single loss. He himself was with the *Hessa* on 29 missions.

After the war, the fisherman was wary of sailing on the sea. This was the result of forty sorties over the North Sea. Yet in the little island community far out in the sea there was no alternative. He had to return to the sea. It was the only means of livelihood.

Even now, more than sixty years after the fishing boat traffic was at its worst, the ageing fisherman on Bulandet still experiences nightmares and painful dreams from his days as skipper on the unusual military vessels.

– Horrible that it's not possible to forget. It never leaves you. Olai Hillersøy's father and three brothers were arrested and punished by the Germans as a direct result of his involvement in the Shetland Bus.

«We waged war from
fishing boats»

«I knew my mother was praying for me»

Johannes Økland was a perfect candidate for service in the military traffic over the North Sea. He was young and had been a fisherman since his confirmation. What's more, he was from an island community in which movement in and out of the country was particularly common. This meant that he was familiar with the places they were going to, and that he knew the people who would be receiving the agents and weapons.

His first trip to Norway went home to the pier at Øklandsvågen – just a few minutes from where he lived. The people they were to contact were neighbours and good friends.

– We landed a couple of agents and some boxes of equipment, but I didn't risk going ashore to meet my family. It was too risky.

The young fisherman, specially trained in marksmanship and sabotage, never had direct contact with his parents despite the fact that he constantly travelled to their island realm in Hordaland. He was often tempted to drop by just to let them know he was alright. His mother, father, and many siblings had not heard from him since he had left for England. They didn't even know if he had survived the journey that stormy night in November of 1941. But the next-to-oldest son knew that if the occupiers discovered he had visited them, his entire family would be punished – this he did not want to hazard.

Nevertheless, Johannes was able to let his family know he was among the living. Through the contact person in the local resistance group, he sent greetings accompanied with an entire roll of shredded tobacco for his father. In this manner his mother and father learned that their twenty-year-old son was sailing back and forth over the North Sea.

Finally they knew what he was doing – and from that day on Johannes also knew that, home at the kitchen table in Bømlo, his mother sat praying for him.

In gratitude for his having sent word, she sent two books about Jesus to him through the local contact person. The next time Johannes arrived in Bømlo with a load of weapons, he received the books along with greetings from his mother.

– It must have been an act of Providence that it all went so well, says the fisherman who completed more than fifty tours over the North Sea.

Name: Johannes Kristensen Olaus Økland
Born: 08.08.1921
Place of birth: Øklandsvågen on Bømlo, Hordaland
Residence: Urangsvåg on Bømlo, Hordaland

Joined the Shetland Bus and completed more than fifty missions to Norway.

«We were shot to bits»

– Larsen had shrapnel in his thigh, Clausen had been hit in the stomach, Enoksen was riddled with bullets, Vika's foot was shot off, and Færøy was so cut up he couldn't stand. I didn't realize that I'd been shot myself until my foot became warm from the blood running down in my boot.

Johannes Kalve, with his sturdy fisherman's hands, relates one of the many missions he went on with Leif Larsen and the rest of the Shetland Bus Men during the war. The crew of the armed fishing boat *Bergholm* were on their way back to Shetland when they were attacked by two aircraft. The cutter was shot so full of holes it sank. One of their mates died in the lifeboat. Only three of the original crew of eight was able to row. The ragged warriors rowed for four days and four nights before reaching safety and friends.

The old fisherman from Bakkasund, furthest north in Austevoll, doesn't use grand words to describe his experiences from two generations ago. Rather than elaborate, he understates. Rather than mention, he lets it slide.

He feels at home on the rocky slopes facing the open sea. Only a little limp on one side reveals that the hefty man with the peaceful temperament has been shot at – has been hunted by the enemy. It is not difficult to understand why he was one of Shetlands-Larsen's most trusted men. Which was why Larsen chose to include Kalve on a top secret, daring raid to Trondheim Fjord to sink the battleship *Tirpitz*. But the sabotage failed, and their only escape route was over the mountain to Sweden.

Once again Kalve clashed with fierce enemies – both German soldiers and the Norwegian climate. The first enemy used bullets. The second let them taste bitter cold, deep snow, slashing winds, and gruelling toil on empty stomachs. Yet the robust purse-seine fisherman made it over to the Swedish side and also back to the base in Shetland also that time.

– I wrapped my shirt around my head and lay under a pine tree until daylight. The next day I was in Sweden, says the hardy chap who was involved in two of the most dramatic shipwrecks of the entire North Sea Traffic.

Name: Johannes Rasmussen Kalve
Born: 28.08.1919
Place of birth: Kalve in Austevoll, Hordaland
Residence: Bakkasund in Austevoll, Hordaland

One of the Shetland Bus warriors who crossed back and forth over the North Sea.

Name: Peder Severinsen Godø
Born: 22.04.1913
Place of birth: Godøy in Giske, Møre and Romsdal
Residence: Godøy in Giske, Møre and Romsdal

One of the warriors in the Shetland Bus who were completely dependent on good people in Norway.

– Without all the helping hands we could never have done our job. All along the Norwegian coast people lent us support.

Peder S. Godø remembers the thousands of women and men who risked their lives merely by speaking with him and the other agents who came to Norway by night. Many were established contacts – others were there by chance, helpers who were just at the right place at the right time. The Shetland Bus was completely dependent on such support: people who could receive weapons deliveries and distribute them further to the home forces.

Teodor Myrvåg and his family on Værlandet, on the outer fringes of Sunnfjord, were among those who provided such helping hands. Someone who had crossed the North Sea had given Myrvågen's name as a trustworthy person in that part of the country. One April day in 1942, the fishing boat *Jakk* turned up, fully loaded with weapons. There was only one house on that side of the island, so the boat pulled all the way up to the quay. The 46-year-old man of the house and his sons had dug a large hole behind the house. There they hid the cache and covered it with sod and heather.

– I will never forget the cooked cod we were served by his wife. Only she and a little girl were home when we arrived. So we sat down at the kitchen table for a regal meal, says Peder S. Godø.

Sixty years have passed since the dinner on Værlandet. The war veteran now lives in his childhood home on Godøy – the same house from which he departed an October evening in 1941, leaving the following message on his bed: «Leaving. Won't be back until Norway is free.» Two generations have grown up since that time, but the memories of the war won't leave the old fisherman. He still wakes up wondering how things went for the people he encountered along the coast.

– I particularly remember the thirteen- or fourteen-year-old girl on Værlandet who was so very sceptical of us strangers.

Since that time he has often thought about the girl and her family. He wonders who they were and what happened to them. I can report that I have just met the same girl. Her name is Gudrun. At that time she was 14 years old. Now she is 75. Both her father and her brothers were taken by the Germans not long after the memorable fish dinner in 1945, but the girl survived, and has since married a skipper in Florø.

– Did you really speak with her? It could be interesting to see her again …

«We met so many
good people»

«Shetlands-Larsen
took my boat»

– We knew where the boat had gone. Many of those who crossed over to England took boats here in this district.

Ingvald Søvik is referring to the October day in 1942 when he discovered that his fishing boat, the *Arthur*, had disappeared from its moorings in Søvik, north of Ålesund. He immediately realised what had happened to it. The coastal fisherman knew that refugees were taking boats in order to cross the North Sea, but Ingvald had no idea that the boat from the little hamlet had sailed into the history books with one of the nation's greatest heroes behind the helm.

Only after the war did Ingvald find out what had happened with his boat. None other than Shetlands-Larsen and the fisherman's own neighbour, Palmer Bjørnøy, had taken the 60-foot fishing boat. Larsen and Bjørnøy had been on a mission further north on the coast, but their converted fishing boat, the *Nordsjøen*, had foundered after they had finished laying out mines. For five and a half days the crew travelled by foot, rowboat, and car to get to Søvik in Haram. They knew that there they could find help to make it back to Shetland. The story has it that the shipwrecked warriors had two boats to choose from, but the choice fell on the *Arthur* because only two bachelors owned it.

– The day before the boat was taken I wondered if I should take the fuel injector home with me. It would then be impossible to start the motor. But I didn't, and the next day the boat was gone.

Ingvald and his cousin Reidar had used the boat for long-line fishing during the summer and for the herring catch in the winter, in addition to taking the odd freight job. In Shetland the fishing boat was converted to a war boat. The cutter was exceptionally seaworthy and soon became the favourite boat of Leif Larsen – «Shetlands-Larsen».

Boat M192B made many successful trips carrying agents and weapons to the Norwegian coast. It was even selected for a top-secret special assignment in autumn 1943, when the Shetland Bus attempted to sink the battleship *Tirpitz* in Trondheim Fjord. The sabotage attempt failed, and the Shetland Bus had had to scuttle the boat. There ended military service for the fishing boat from Søvik.

– The boat was our means of earning a living, so work was harder without it, but we managed. Now we're proud of the role our boat has played in history. It has earned a place in world history.

Over time, anger and frustration have turned into respect and pride. Ingvald and Reidar got their boat back after the war, and they have now read all the books describing the heroic missions the *Arthur* took part in. The cutter, raised by the Germans during the war, continued in service as a fishing boat until it was retired and buried at the bottom of Volda Fjord in the 1970's.

Name: Ingvald Alfred Søvik
Born: 30.04.1914
Place of birth:
Søvik in Haram,
Møre and Romsdal
Residence:
Søvik in Haram,
Møre and Romsdal

The Shetland Bus Men took his fishing boat and converted it into a war boat.

Name: Odd Meling
Born: 27.06.1914
Place of birth: Melingsvågen
on Bømlo, Hordaland
Residence: Haugesund,
Rogaland

Name: Marie Meling
Maiden name: Svendsen
Born: 06.04.1915
Place of birth: Sønstebøvågen
on Bømlo, Hordaland
Residence: Haugesund,
Rogaland

The married couple were contacts for the Shetland boats.

Odd and Marie Meling were contacts for the boats from Shetland. When the couple expected a boat, they made their own lighthouse – they kept the light on in the west-facing window of their living room so the crew could find their way into Melingsvågen («Meling bay») on Bømlo, Sunnhordland.

– We had been waiting all night and were very tired. In the first grey light the fishing boat appeared. The skipper began talking about the flywheel, and I answered cylinder head. This is how I knew he was the right man.

Odd is referring to his first encounter with Shetlands-Larsen, a few days before Christmas of 1942. It was neither the first nor the last time he would meet boats in the shuttle traffic between the British Isles and the islands of western Norway. Already in the summer of 1940, he sent his own fishing smack over the North Sea, carrying the family of the British consul in Stavanger and the royal aide-de-camp. The following autumn the smack returned with one of the refugees, now a trained agent. From that day on, Odd was a contact man for the secret traffic.

At home sat his wife Marie. Well aware of his activities, she more than once took care of the guests who had either arrived from Shetland or who were heading in that direction. No one was to know of the couple's involvement in the dangerous traffic, but this was no simple matter with three generations living under the same roof.

– People probably had some idea of what was going on out here, but no one ever spoke about it. They pretended as if they neither saw nor heard, remembers Marie.

She thinks about her sister, who came to visit one time when one of the Shetland men was staying in the attic. He had been warned to keep still, but the man was large and the bed small. As a result he often had to shift around, and the creaking noises were clearly audible in the living room below. Her sister didn't say a word. Nor did Odd's father, despite the fact that he had begun to wonder why his son never caught fish when he went out fishing.

When Odd went «fishing», he was often meeting a boat, receiving a load of weapons, or accompanying an agent who was to return to Shetland. The contact man remembers one of these trips especially well. It was in November 1941. Agent Bernhard Håvardsholm was waiting to return to Shetland. London had informed them that the boat should arrive within four days, so the pair in Melingsvågen kept the light burning in the living room. On the third night they were roused by a crowd of navy seamen in their bedroom. Once again, the Shetland Bus had found its way to «Kjeilo» – the little farm on Melingsvågen. But this time their boat was named *Blia*. It never arrived in Shetland. The agent and forty-two others vanished without a trace into the waves.

– There was an air of excitement in the house when we were expecting a boat, but we tried to live our lives as normally as possible.

For three years, Odd and Marie helped to keep the lines over the North Sea open, but in May 1943 the light in the living room window went out. Odd had been arrested and was nearly beaten to death by the Germans before landing in a concentration camp. Marie was let off, but had to live with the pain of a thwarted man for almost sixty years.

«We kept a light on in the window
so the boats could find us»

«I had to get out of the country»

From the summer of 1940, when three English soldiers lay in hiding in Skorpa after the first battles in Norway had ended, Gerhard Skorpen held the North Sea connection open. The little island with five small farms, located furthest out in Herøy in Sunnmøre, is said to be the only point that managed to maintain contact over the North Sea throughout the entire war. Skorpa became a lifeline connecting occupied Norway and free Great Britain.

Name: Gerhard Skorpen
Born: 26.06.1918
Place of birth: Skorpa
in Herøy,
Møre and Romsdal
Residence: Leinøy
in Herøy,
Møre and Romsdal

Contact for people arriving from Shetland. From 1944 himself a member of the Shetland Bus.

Together with his neighbour and uncle, Johan Skorpen, Gerhard Skorpen helped English soldiers and other refugees safely over to Great Britain. Before the end of the war there would be many such visitors in the little community.

In his early twenties, the young man became the contact person for secret agents who landed in Norway in order to establish radio stations, carry out sabotage, or train leaders for the resistance movement. Here the specially-trained agents were dropped off, and here they were picked up when their job was done. In Skorpa's narrow straights boats from Shetland arrived loaded with weapons, and boats with resistance workers waited to be picked up by the Shetland Bus. Agents knew that if they made it to Skorpa they were safe – whether their journey was further into land or across the North Sea.

Many know the story about Shetlands-Larsen who was sunk by artillery fire off the Norwegian coast. Less well-known is that among the anonymous rescuers were small-time fishers and farmers Gerhard and Johan Skorpen, who sheltered Leif Larsen and the rest of the *Berholm* crew in a cow shed on Skorpa. Four days later the message had reached the other side of the North Sea, and the crew was picked up by a boat from Shetland.

Towards the end of 1943, Gerhard Skorpen had to go into hiding himself. He had attracted the attention of the German security police and had to get out of the country. Their 27-foot

fishing boat disappeared from the island, and both Gerhard and his fiancée Sina Dragsund were reported missing. They had disappeared en route to Nordmøre. While their death certificates were being penned in Norway, Sina and Gerhard were going ashore in Shetland. A few days later they married in London. Not long afterwards, Gerhard was back on Skorpa. This time he came in uniform and by sea; Gerhard had become part of the same Shetland Bus he

had so many times welcomed to Skorpa. Now it was his uncle who welcomed them.

Gerhard returns to the island on which he grew up together with his mother and grandmother, and where he later settled with his own family. Today there is no longer life here; only holidaymakers come here now. The rest of the year the houses stand empty. In 1970, Gerhard Skorpen was the last to move off the island.

«We were nice to the
Norwegians»

In the Village's Embrace

Once dialects from Godøy, Bulandet, and other Norwegian coastal settlements were common in the streets.
From the wharf one heard the tock-tocks of the Møre cutters and the sharp blows of ship's carpenters.

On the spartan slipway, machine guns in oil drums were mounted on Norwegian boats.
In the red warehouse slept Norwegian fishermen in navy uniforms.
On the main street, many a soldier found consolation in the hands of a young girl.
And the four-hundred-year-old castle concealed tons of weapons and ammunition.

The boys in the Shetland Bus made the little village their base.
The people of the village took them in as their own.
Today only memories remain.

Scalloway, Shetland

Name: Wilhelmina «Minnie» Margaret Pearson
Maiden name: Davidson
Born: 19.05.1917
Place of birth: Scalloway, Shetland
Residence: Scalloway, Shetland

Scalloway girl who will never forget the Norwegian boys.

«We were nice to the Norwegian boys»

– We knew that they were going to war and might never return. So we were nice to the Norwegian boys, says Minnie Davidson (married name Pearson).

Minnie was one of the Scalloway girls in their early twenties who became enamoured of the Norwegian boys who used their little village in Shetland as their base. She was the same age as the soldiers from Norway and thought it exciting to meet the amiable fellows from the other side of the North Sea.

As the daughter of the local cobbler, she saw much more of the soldiers than most others. The uniformed Norwegian fishers and seamen came to her house to deliver shoes that needed mending, and a few days later they came back to pick them up. While they waited, the Davidson family usually served them a cup of tea.

The women in Scalloway – young and old – did what they could to assist the Norwegian soldiers who were fighting to liberate Norway. They invited them to dinner or for a cup of tea, and sewed on insignia or repaired uniforms without asking where the soldiers had been. They knew the Norwegians' assignments were secret.

– The boys from Norway behaved politely. They were kind, wonderful fellows – and they were such good dancers, remembers Minnie about the men she met at the local café on the hill or at the dance down by the harbour.

The girls in Scalloway felt angst and fear every time they saw the boats set sail for war missions to Norway. When the soldiers returned safely, the girls were filled with relief.

– When the boys came back from Norway they sometimes took us in their arms and lifted us up in the middle of the street. I think they were happy to be back, says the woman who also met many soldiers who never made it back.

Minnie has become an elderly woman – a widow after her Shetland husband but with a lifelong friendship to Norwegian men. At home are Christmas cards from the entire coast of Norway and an address book full of names. Minnie Pearson will never forget the Norwegians – and the Norwegian boys will never forget the girls in Scalloway.

«We knew they
were going to
Norway to carry
out sabotage»

Name: William Cecil Duncan
Born: 07.08.1924
Place of birth: Burra Isle, Shetland
Residence: Scalloway, Shetland

Worked at the slipway in Scalloway where the Shetland Bus had their base the last three years of the war.

Cecil Duncan was an engineer and machinist with William Moore and Sons when the Norwegian men moved into the machine shop in Scalloway. The fleet of militarised fishing boats had become so extensive that the unusual division needed its own workshop.

Seventeen years old and with one year behind him as an apprentice, the young man would acquire first-hand knowledge of the Norwegian smacks and cutters – a knowledge that served him well when the same boats returned on more peaceful errands after the war. Cecil often worked with the Norwegian machinists who maintained the peculiar dunk-dunk motors, and he became acquainted with many of the young men who travelled back and forth to Norway. Many of them never returned.

- We didn't know much about their activities, but we did know they were going to Norway to carry out sabotage. We never spoke about what we saw.

Two generations later, Cecil still lives with a view of his erstwhile workplace. He worked 48 years at the slipway and workshop in Scalloway.

The slip from 1942 is still in operation, and the office building where he met his wife still shares a wall with the little slipway where everything from small fishing boats to enormous sub-chasers were pulled up from the sea. From the shop we hear the sounds of drilling. The retired machinist's thoughts drift back to the time when, as an apprentice, he took part in fashioning armour plate as well as barrels which would camouflage machine guns on the fishing boats. In the evenings he made the crowbars that the secret agents would carry with them on their sabotage missions.

– I'll never forget the Norwegians. We got along very well and became good friends. They were fishers – just like the people here.

«The men were worn out when they came back from Norway»

As a maid at Flemington, the Shetland Bus's headquarters, 19-year-old Betty Polson (married name Jamieson) was nearer the centre of events than she realised.

Name: Betty Jamieson
Maiden name: Polson
Born: 21.01.1924
Place of birth:
Whalsay, Shetland
Residence: Scalloway,
Shetland

Housemaid at Flemington – the headquarters of the Shetland Bus.

In the isolated mansion in the middle of Shetland, the leader for the Shetland Bus received only the most important guests. Here agents came to rest after assignments in Norway, and here skippers came to plan their next tour. Here the top-secret plans for sinking the German battleship Tirpitz were discussed, and here Crown Prince Olav lunched when he visited Shetland in 1942. A guest once came here disguised as a priest, and people regularly arrived with suitcases full of poisons and explosives.

– We knew that we mustn't ever say anything about what we saw or heard. Everything was hush-hush, says Betty. She remembers that the Norwegian couple at Flemington never taught their five-year-old son Norwegian for fear he would understand what the adults were talking about.

The sprawling Flemington estate lies nestled in the peaceful valley of Weisdale – twenty minutes' drive north of Lerwick. The location is renowned for its grand old trees in the otherwise treeless island region.

Already in 1940, British authorities began to use the house as a planning base for military traffic between Shetland and Norway. When Betty arrived in Flemington in early 1943, Arthur William Sclater was leader of the special division.

He was responsible for both the Norwegian and British crews involved in the traffic, while his Norwegian-born wife Alice supervised the welfare of the Norwegian agents.

– Some of the men looked completely worn out when they came here to rest, remembers Betty about the Norwegian agents who stopped at Flemington while preparing themselves for new missions to Norway.

She herself lived in the attic with two other housemaids. The trio were responsible for maintenance of the peculiar residence in which mounted deer heads, birds, and large fish adorned the drawing room walls. In addition to house cleaning and making beds, the young women tended the fire of coal and peat in the hundred-year-old house. Every evening dinner was prepared for the small family, the agents, and the other guests, and at weekends there were often dinner parties. She remembers many of the figures who came and went.

– When Leif Larsen came there was always a lot of laughter and merriment, reminisces the maid who will never forget the agent from Ålesund who turned the house upside down to find a bottle of rum, or the dinner guests who loudly discussed top-secret plans.

Back on the large estate that after the war received the name «Kergord», Betty notices how high the sycamore by the driveway has become, and she sees that the strange tree «monkey puzzle» still stands the garden.

– The well-tended gardens reminded Mrs. Rogers of her home in England, says Betty, without noticing that she still uses the false name assumed by the Sclater family during the war.

«It was top-secret, but we saw everything»

Ten-year-old Gilbert «Gibbie» Johnson knew that something unusual was going on in the large stone manor on Lunna. More than once the young boy had seen trucks arriving at night and Norwegian fishing boats arriving and leaving.

He himself lived just over the bay with his mother, father, two younger brothers, and a sister. From the kitchen window they had a good view of the first clandestine base of the Shetland Bus – a half hour's drive north of Lerwick.

– We didn't know what was going on there, but we heard shooting, remembers Gibbie about this period in the untamed, remote neighbourhood, sixty years earlier. Later he found out that the shots came from the Shetland Bus, who were killing time by shooting rabbits, seals, and anything else that stirred in the bay in the northeast of mainland Shetland.

Gibbie had been given explicit instructions to stay away from Lunna, but one October day in 1942 he could no longer control himself. Together with a school friend and his two younger brothers, he bicycled over to take a closer look at the mysterious place. At this point the base, with the entire Shetland Bus and all the boats, had been moved to Scalloway, but that Saturday something so top-secret was taking place at Lunna that even most of the Norwegian boat-soldiers didn't know about it.

– We saw a man come right up out of the sea. When he climbed onto the pier we saw them lift three or four curious machines out of the water and wheel them into the boathouse. Gibbie and his friends lay completely still behind a stone fence.

Monday morning, a military officer came to the school. He wanted to know who had been out at Lunna on Saturday. The angry officer made fierce attempts to convince the boys that they hadn't seen anything, and the two friends were severely warned not to speak about what they had seen.

Only many years later did Gibbie learn what he had seen that Saturday in October of 1942. The British had just invented a type of miniature submarine to be controlled by divers. The Shetland Bus was to transport these machines to the Norwegian coast on a fishing boat. There the specially trained divers would use them to attach explosives to the hull of the massive battle ship Tirpitz, moored in Trondheim Fjord.

The plan was so immense and top-secret that only the highest-ranking officers knew about it. The last exercises before the mission to Norway were therefore held at deserted Lunna. But nobody had figured on the inquisitive schoolboys who saw the whole thing.

Gibbie Johnson is still one of the nearest neighbours to Lunna House. It is serene and beautiful here when the weather allows it, and wild and tempestuous when nature shows its power. One seldom meets people at this outpost. Only the occasional busload of Norwegian tourists in search of the top-secret base find their way here now.

– People up here are proud that Lunna played a role in the war, says the retired businessman who has built up a small empire based on salmon and other fish from the region.

Name: Gilbert «Gibbie» Johnson
Born: 21.11.1930
Place of birth: Vidlin, Shetland
Residence: Vidlin, Shetland

Neighbour boy who saw things he shouldn't have at the secret base, Lunna.

«I longed horribly
for home»

Encounter With a World City

The almost one-hundred-year-old railway station King's Cross was the refugees'
first encounter with London – the city of which they had dreamt. A symbol of freedom and courage.
If the rail journey through Scotland and England was indescribable, the sea of people
and the architecture of King's Cross left most breathless.

Royal Victoria Patriotic School. From the tower of the majestic school,
England's guardian angel St. George extends his welcome. The lofty Victorian building, for eighty years
a hospital, children's home, and school, became a provisional home for war refugees.
No one will forget the gravity of the interrogations here.

The new nation was exhilarating. Those who made the journey to England were soon as familiar with Trafalgar Square
and Piccadilly Circus as they were with their own fishing fields at home. Yet while the temptations of the metropolis
were many, homesickness was a constant companion.

They came from the smallest settlements to one of the world's largest cities.
But they knew they would be returning home.
This was the reason they had left.

London, England

WAY OUT &
CENTRAL LINE PLATFORMS 1 & 2

Name: Arne Bjørsvik
Born: 16.08.1910
Place of birth: Bjørsvik
in Osterfjorden,
Hordaland
Residence: Grays in
Essex, England

**Norwegian
refugee who
married an
English girl and
settled in «the
land of freedom».**

«Everything was different in London»

Like most of the refugees, Arne Bjørsvik hailed from a small settlement in western Norway. He had lived in Oslo and Bergen for brief periods, but nothing could compare with what he encountered in London in April 1945.

The metropolis teemed with life. What made the greatest impression on him was the traffic and chaos in the streets. In Bergen, where he had been living the past few years, there were far more horses than cars. In London, the opposite was true. In the middle of Piccadilly Circus he saw enormous double-decker buses wallowing through traffic, jostling shoulders with small trucks and people pushing wagon carts. The 34-year-old furniture maker from Osterfjorden also noticed that the city was full of people from foreign countries. Prior to arriving in London, the only dark-skinned person he had encountered was the boy who sold newspapers in Bergen, but here in this megalopolis there were dark-skinned people everywhere.

– Everything was new, says the man who had never before been abroad.

The bombardment of the British capital was over by the time Arne Bjørsvik moved into the Norwegian Shaftesbury Hotel in the centre of what we now call the West End. The devastating results of the German bombers were everywhere. Vast sections of the city lay in ruins. In the city centre gaped the demolished hulks of churches and other large buildings.

Arne Bjørsvik didn't know a word of English, yet he soon found a way to become acquainted with the city that seemed so overwhelming to him. Four million inhabitants – this was much larger than the entire population of Norway at the time.

– We would take the Underground as far as we could. Then we hopped on another train going in the opposite direction. We did this every Sunday, all day. We only came up for something to eat – and then we went down again.

Shaftesbury Hotel in the middle of London. Arne Bjørsvik stands outside what was once his home. Sixty years have passed. The city has long-since recovered and seems new compared with that time. In his nineties, he still allows himself to be impressed over how remarkable the city has become – despite the fact that he has lived most of his life only a half-hour's train trip outside London. The office worker from the Norwegian Seamen's Department in London had met an English girl who spoke Norwegian. After the war they married and settled down outside London. Yet an Englishman he will never be. He has held as tightly to his Norwegian passport as he has to the «ø» in his last name.

– English people still think I'm odd for not going to the pub, says the elderly temperance advocate who left Norway for life in a foreign land.

«Everyone waited for news from home»

London was where exiled Norwegians congregated. From all parts of Great Britain, Norwegian women and men made their way to the bustling capital whenever they had free time. Many came all the way from Shetland, seamen came from the British harbour towns, and soldiers with the Norwegian flag on their right shoulder arrived from the busy airports outside London. On overfilled trains they pulled into the vast railway stations where they were swallowed up in the crowds. The next day they might report to a military office, but first they could relax at a hotel.

The lounges at the County and the Shaftesbury Hotels, situated in the heart of the great metropolis, were usually one of the main motivations for coming to London. At these places Norwegians could hope to encounter someone from their own district or hear the latest news from home. The man who could provide them with this information was Per Dimmen from Ulsteinvik – the unofficial news correspondent for Norwegians in London.

– I always knew which boats had come over and which people were on them. We also received news about events in Norway. There was always a stir when I had some news from home I could pass on.

Twenty-year-old Per Dimmen worked in the so-called «I-office», the intelligence office of the Norwegian Department of Defence. He had worked there since crossing the North Sea on a fishing boat in the summer of 1941. He interviewed refugees from Norway to find out what they knew about conditions where they came from. What kinds of German facilities

were there? Did they know about any dangerous Nazis? Per Dimmen was responsible for keeping all this information in a card file.

Everyone waited for word from home and the latest news was spread through the lounges of the County Hotel after working hours. Here people sat and waited for Per Dimmen so they could hear the latest from Norway. Have you heard anything from home? Have my relatives come over? The questions hailed on the uniformed man when he met acquaintances.

– Often I could relate that I had just spoken with someone from their community or a relative who had come over.

He received news of his own family in the same fashion. A number of fathers from Ulsteinvik had been taken hostage after their sons crossed to England. His father was one of them, according to the news he received. Alone at home sat his mother with two young daughters.

– I was very depressed and thought a great deal about my family at home. I cried at Christmas and felt miserable being in a foreign country.

Two generations after the end of the war Per Dimmen is back in industry town Ulsteinvik, after many years spent in other areas of the county. On the pier from which he fled together with 16 others from his community, his thoughts turn to his years in London.

– Only after the war have I come to understand how vital these small crumbs of information from Norway were for us living in foreign countries.

Name: Per Dimmen
Born: 14.03.1921
Place of birth:
Ulsteinvik
in Sunnmøre,
Møre and Romsdal
Residence: Ulsteinvik
in Sunnmøre,
Møre and Romsdal

Employed in the intelligence office in London, and a vital source of news from home.

Name: Karen "Kari" Stave
Maiden name: Fæstø
Born: 16.11.1917
Place of birth: Ålesund, Møre and Romsdal
Residence: Ålesund, Møre and Romsdal

Fled with her husband, but pined so much for home that her life in exile seemed a nightmare.

«I missed home so much»

Karen Fæstø (married name Stave) missed Norway so much that her four years in exile seemed like a nightmare. When she returned to Norway in late 1945, she vowed never to leave Ålesund again. She has kept her promise – with the exception of a few brief holidays.

– I was often alone, and not a day passed when I didn't pine for Ålesund. The loneliness frayed my nerves and I lost one-and-a-half stone, says the retiree about her war years in exile.

Twenty-seven years old, Karen left for England with her fiancée. But life in a foreign land proved a solitary affair. Only four days after their marriage in a Seaman's Church in London, her husband was sent to Canada to be trained as an aeroplane mechanic. Karen was left in the big city – alone. Seven months later her husband returned, but three weeks later he was sent to Iceland. This time she was allowed to accompany him, but also here she was often by herself. In the basement apartment of a tea kitchen outside Reykjavik, Karen sat alone, thinkingabout her husband out fighting the war.

– London was the worst. I was very lonely there. On Iceland I at least had an aunt – and then my daughter was born. That made life much better.

The story of the fish merchant's daughter from Ålesund is not so unlike the stories of many other women who crossed over to England. Many were isolated in a foreign land – far from family and friends. For many the homesickness was overwhelming, but there was no turning back.

Today Karen lives in the middle of the Sunnmøre city. She has been here since the end of the war. Nothing can induce her to leave this city celebrated for its Art-Nouveau architecture, but she often recalls the day in 1941 when she left her hometown. Things were different then. Norway was occupied and you were expected to go to England to take part in the fight. Many of her friends had taken that route, and now she would follow with her husband. But it was not easy. Karen remembers how she studied the family pictures before finally packing some clothes and leaving with her husband and 58 other refugees. It can't be for long, she reassured herself. It turned out to be four years of loneliness.

– I wouldn't do it again. Four years of the best part of my life. No, that is an experience I could have well done without.

Name: Ingvald Olai Sulen
Born: 04.07.1913
Place of birth:
Fedje, Hordaland
Residence:
Buckie, Scotland

Came to Buckie as a refugee and never returned to Norway.

Norwegian Ingvald Sulen lives in a cement-grey terrace house in the northern Scotland village of Buckie. The almost ninety-year-old man sits in a wheelchair and has not been out of his house for many months. With some reluctance he joins us outside for a few photographs.

Ingvald has lived twice as long here in the little fishing village as home on Fedje in Hordaland. The explanation is found sixty years earlier. In 1941 he left home as the skipper of the *Alf* – the boat he owned with his three brothers. The 28-year-old wished to escape to freedom by crossing over to Shetland together with 26 other refugees. After the obligatory trip to London to be approved as a «good Norwegian», he continued to Buckie where he found employment both as a fisherman and in a workshop.

The Norwegian spent the war years in Buckie – the village which had become a home for between 300 to 400 Norwegian fishers and others who hailed from the Norwegian coast. He rented a room with the Brown family, where their 16-year-old daughter caught his eye. She became pregnant.

– I decided to take full responsibility for my actions. We married and I lived in Buckie the rest of my life.

When the war ended, most Norwegians went back to Norway. Not Ingvald. He bought a house and settled down with his 15-years-younger wife Annie Marie and their daughter Britha, born in 1944.

Ingvald has become a living reminder of the Norwegian community that existed in Buckie during the war. Many of the refugees who arrived in Shetland in smacks and other fishing boats were sent on to Buckie, where they abandoned their boats in the harbour and continued by train to London. Quite a few of these refugees retraced their steps to the little harbour village that had contributed its own boats and men to the war. In 1942, the Norwegian authorities established a slipway and workshop in Buckie; many Norwegian fishermen and seamen found work here. Others made their way fishing. Soon Buckie had its own Norwegian consulate, doctor, reading room, and its own club bearing the name «Buckie 1940 Norwegian Club». Buckie had become a Norwegian exile town, and wartime Buckie was often referred to as «Little Norway».

– I don't know anymore if I'm Norwegian or Scottish, but I've kept my Norwegian passport, says Ingvald Sulen in a blend of Norwegian and the special Buckie dialect.

«She became pregnant, so
I settled down for good»

Name: Jane Geddes Cowie
Maiden name: Murray
Born: 20.10.1917
Place of birth: Inverness, Scotland
Residence: Buckie, Scotland

Remembers the Norwegian community in North Scotland during the war.

– The arrival of peace was bittersweet for many Buckie girls. The good news meant that the Norwegian boys were going back to Norway, and many romances would have a sudden end.

Jane Geddes Cowie reminisces about the Norwegians who lived in Buckie during the war. She knows many women in the fishing village in North Scotland still dream about a Norwegian boyfriend they never saw again.

Jane stops outside a brick building on the village's main street. It is here the offices of the Norwegian consulate were located during the war. Jane was the consul's assistant. In this building she registered all the Norwegian refugees who came to live in Buckie, and it was here she took care of the girls who never heard from their boyfriends again. It was also here that she organised return trips for several hundred Norwegians when the war ended.

– We will never forget the Norwegian boys. They were wonderful fellows – and more polite than our own.

With the armistice, the men left with promises to return for their Scottish girlfriends. Most never came back. Jane had learned a little Norwegian, and after the war many young Buckie girls came to her to have their love letters from Norway translated. But the assistant at the consulate didn't translate everything. She realised that they would never meet again, and wished to spare the girls some of the details. One girl was so head-over-heels she packed all her expensive silverware and a coffee service in a large crate that her boyfriend took home on a fishing boat to Norway. The North Sea divided them for good and she never saw him again. As a result, there is a family in western Norway that has been drinking coffee out of a Buckie coffee service for sixty years.

At the time of the war, Buckie was a busy fishing village. In many ways it resembled similar settlements in Norway, which made it easier for Norwegians to feel at home. Today, Buckie is a sleepy village with 6000 inhabitants. The fishing industry has all but disappeared and unemployment is high. No traces are left of the Norwegian slipway that employed up to seventy people. But the memories of «the Norwegian Buckie» are still poignant for the village residents.

«The peace took their boyfriends»

«Every evening they
came down to hear
their national song on
the radio»

Name: Margaret Hunter
Maiden name: Smith
Born: 08.02.1935
Place of birth: Portessie on the outskirts of Buckie, Scotland
Residence: Banff, Scotland

Young girl who remembers the exiled Norwegians living in her home.

For sixty years now, letters and postcards have criss-crossed the North Sea carrying greetings from two coastal communities that will never forget each other. The Scots think about the Norwegians who made small towns in Scotland their own, and the Norwegian families are eternally grateful to the Scots who so willingly opened their homes.

Margaret Smith (married name Hunter) represents one of the many families in the Buckie region that took a Norwegian family into their home. She was only seven years old when a family from Sogn moved into her home. The encounter with people who had to flee their country brought the war frighteningly close.

– Every evening they came down to hear the Norwegian national song on BBC radio. This made a great impression on us.

The Scottish schoolgirl spent a good deal of time with Norwegian children and learned a little Norwegian. She could count in Norwegian and sing «Silent Night». Now it is all gone. Yet the feeling of closeness to her neighbours on the other side of the sea remains. She has a bag full of pictures, letters, and postcards from Norway. Here are wedding photos, family photos, and Christmas cards bearing greetings from three generations. There is only one hitch – she has forgotten her Norwegian, and it seems as if the Norwegians have forgotten their English.

– Could you translate for me? she inquires, enthusiastic as a child. In this way she finally finds out the «latest news» about who bought a house and who divorced – around Christmas of 1989.

Between 300 and 400 exiled Norwegians settled in Buckie and other villages in North Scotland during the war. Margaret's mother was one of those who opened their homes when the authorities asked for help to shelter the refugees. Those who didn't have extra space instead invited them to dinner on Sundays.

Margaret remembers the Lamrects family from Solund in Sogn, the first to move in. A man, a woman, and their five children. He worked at the Norwegian slipway, as did one of his sons. Another son and daughter were in the Norwegian navy, one boy attended the Norwegian school outside Aberdeen, and the youngest child was home. Later came the Johansen family from Helgeland. There were only four in this family.

The correspondence over the North Sea has proceeded in jumps and starts. Language differences and new generations have complicated communication, but thirteen years ago Bjørg, the neighbour girl Margaret played with during the war, suddenly turned up in Buckie. This set off a new wave of post cards between the two neighbouring countries.

Agents

«There were always agents
at our farm»

A Contact Man is Gone

The garden on the little island was known for its lilacs, hydrangea, and colourful tulips.
And the man of the house was known as an important contact for those who came
from Shetland.

In the kitchen often sat specially-trained agents and radio operators. Under the
cowshed floor was Sten Gun ammunition. On the quay waited cases
to be covered with sand and sent into the fjords.

Today the quay and the cow shed have collapsed.
An owl has moved into the kitchen,
and the well-groomed garden has become a wild imp.
The contact man and his family have left
– for good.

Domba on Hovden, Sogn and Fjordane

«I was a secret agent»

Åsmund Færøy was part of «Polar Bear 4». He was a secret agent with special training in explosives and sabotage.

On a late summer day in 1941, Åsmund left his job as an apprentice at a motor factory on Rubbestadneset in Bømlo, Sunnhordland. He had been bitten by «England fever», and wanted to make the trip over. On 2nd September he accomplished his goal when the fishing boat *Straumøy* pulled quayside in Shetland. A few days later the thirty escapees were assigned to various branches of service. Some entered the merchant marine, while others enlisted in the navy or air force. For the twenty-five-year-old teacher's son from Solund in Sogn, it was the special forces. He would travel back and forth to Norway and operate behind enemy lines. A perilous assignment.

– Angst was part of our daily lives when we were on assignment in Norway.

Åsmund Færøy explains how the secret agents worked. In April 1945 the Shetland Bus put him ashore at Øklandsvågen in Bømlo. With him he had weapons, hand grenades, provisions, and electricity meters – altogether a ton of equipment. People from the local resistance group conveyed him to Stavanger where his assignment was to be carried out. Nobody knew who he was or what he was going to do. Only agent Færøy knew that he had been sent by the anti-sabotage group in the Naval High Command, and that his mission was to prevent destruction of piers and cranes in the event of a German retreat or an Allied invasion.

Name: Åsmund Færøy
Born: 25.07.1916
Place of birth: Solund in Sogn, Sogn and Fjordane
Residence: Haugesund, Rogaland

The agent knew well that he was only a small chip in an immense game. He had learned how to take his own life, and he was prepared to do this – ready to remove a little chip from a momentous contest.

– When I was arrested in Haugesund I searched for my cyanide tablets, but they must have fallen out of my blue jeans during the arrest.

In the prison he tried to hang himself with a belt. This is how he had been trained. Fortunately, the suicide attempt failed, and a few days later the Germans capitulated. When the Allied forces arrived in Stavanger, Åsmund Færøy met them with an English pistol in his jeans pocket. The agent had accomplished his mission and could report that there were no explosives in the quay structures.

Secret agent who operated behind enemy lines.

Name: August Sande
Born: 21.05.1917
Place of birth: Nordbotnen in Bremanger,
Sogn and Fjordane
Residence: Nordbotnen in Bremanger,
Sogn and Fjordane

Assisted Norwegian agents and consequently had to escape to Shetland himself.

August Sande remembers well the September evening in 1943 when three specially-trained soldiers from the Linge company came down from the mountain and asked for help. A boat from Shetland had just landed the Norwegian agents. With each their own kayak, they were to sabotage boats in the shipping lane outside Svelgen. Twenty-six-year-old August Sande, heir to the family farm in the roadless settlement Nordbotn, found himself in the middle of operation «Vestige I».

– We didn't give a thought to the danger. We were just so excited to see three men in Norwegian uniforms that we agreed to help.

In the dark of night, August Sande and neighbour boy Orvald Sletten towed the kayaks, agents, and all their equipment to an inlet in Nordgulen, where they would wait for a suitable ship. Three weeks later the Linge Men made a night attack and attached magnetic mines to a combined transport and supply ship. But the charges went off a whole 25 minutes too early. As a result the Norwegian soldiers once again knocked on the doors to August Sande and Orvald Sletten. By then the agents had sunk their kayaks and hidden their equipment. Now they had to get out to the coast to be fetched back to Shetland. Again August Sande slipped out in the dark with his 25-foot motorboat. This time to transport the agents to

the island Hovden, where an important contact person lived. A few weeks later the Norwegian agents were safe in Shetland.

August Sande is back on the rocky slope where he once concealed the equipment and mines of the saboteurs after they had had to flee the country. From the little hill behind the farm, it is easy to see why the agents chose to put ashore just here. The settlement lies right on the shipping lane near the approach to Frøysjøen. Here they would have had an excellent view of the boats that came and went, at the same time that the mountains offered good hiding places.

– The mines, the machine gun, and various other equipment lay buried here until after the war. But the wireless receiver with the headphones we took home with us so we could hear the news from London, says the fisherman and farmer who was responsible for his mother, a sister, and two brothers while his father was away working on a construction job.

After the departure of the Norwegian agents, the family lived in constant fear of reprisals. One March day in 1945 they saw the outlines of what they had most feared – the Gestapo boat.

– We were at the merchant's on the other side of the fjord, but we were prepared for this possibility. We had arranged with our family that if the Gestapo boat came, they should call us and ask us to buy a loaf of bread.

There was neither bread nor other goods at the family home in Nordbotnen that day. August Sande and Orvald Sletten took off for the mountains where they would wait for a boat that could carry them to Shetland.

«We hid their
equipment in a scree
behind the farm»

«I was a messenger
for one of the
agents»

There is nothing about Reidunn Havnevik (married name Aarsæther) that evinces thoughts of secret agents or spies, but at twenty years of age she was drawn into exactly this kind of work.

She is back outside the house in which she grew up in Ålesund. Uncomfortable memories press in on the eighty-year-old woman. It was here she was arrested after a German spy reported her. Reidunn says that when she was released from prison, she took off and went into hiding, and was taken to Great Britain on a military vessel. The retired teacher explains how she became a runner for one of the secret agents in Norway.

– Karl Johan called and asked if I wanted to «join». I said yes, and bicycled to his house.

It was difficult to say no when Karl Johan, the young man she had had her eye on at upper secondary school, asked for help. With a slight crush, and unaware of what was to come, she agreed to assist her friend.

Karl Johan Aarsæther had just returned from England – via Shetland. He was sent to Norway as a secret agent to spy on the Germans and make reports to London, aided by radio operators and coded messages. He shared the work with, among others, his brother Knut. When one of the brothers needed a break, he was picked up by the Shetland Bus and taken to London. Meanwhile, the other brother took over in Norway. In this manner, the group «Antrum» reported the news from Ålesund until the arrival of peace in May 1945.

The only woman in the group, Reidunn became the agents' message-bearer. She would carry various papers and packages. Her instructions were clear: No questions. Just pick up and deliver. It was also her job to bring fresh bread and the latest news to her boyfriend. He had to move from place to place so the wireless operator wouldn't be discovered, and she subsequently found herself enlisting both rowboats and her bicycle to reach the different hide-outs.

– They needed a woman who could get through the German check-points. I smiled prettily and always got through the guards at the bridge, says the agents' message-girl and girlfriend, still wearing the diamond ring Karl Johan brought back from England. They were married in London. in 1944.

Name: Reidunn Astrid Havnevik Aarsæther
Maiden name: Havnevik
Born: 23.11.1920
Place of birth: Ålesund, Møre and Romsdal
Residence: Ålesund, Møre and Romsdal

Girlfriend and message-bearer for one of the secret agents.

Name: Ottar Inge Karl Giske
Born: 22.11.1933
Place of birth: Bjørgeholmen in Ellingsøyfjorden, Møre and Romsdal
Residence: Bjørgeholmen in Ellingsøyfjorden, Møre and Romsdal

Name: Hans Magne Giske
Born: 23.06.1931
Place of birth: Bjørgeholmen in Ellingsøyfjorden, Møre and Romsdal
Residence: Ålesund, Møre and Romsdal

Name: Irma Mary Giske Olsen
Maiden name: Giske
Born: 07.07.1928
Place of birth: Bjørgeholmen in Ellingsøyfjorden, Møre and Romsdal
Residence: Ålesund, Møre and Romsdal

Siblings who remember the agents who were always at their farm.

For the three children in the Giske family, living on the secluded island of Bjørgeholmen in a fjord near Ålesund, close contact with secret agents was an everyday occurrence. Their small farm provided shelter for strangers with radio transmitters and hid cases of weapons and ammunitions.

– The radio operator lived in the loft of the storehouse, and the antennae was hidden in a rope that led over to the hay barn. Ottar often sat watching the agents when they contacted London. Headsets, encryption, Morse code, and special messages were exciting stuff for the youngest on the farm.

– We were constantly going to the coast to fetch cases of weapons and explosives from Shetland. The oldest, Hans, accompanied his father on the fishing boat and helped with the heavy work of manoeuvring the boxes into the hay barn at home.

– The agents taught me how to swim. Irma remembers how the Norwegian wireless operators were like uncles in their family. It was also her job to carry letters and messages into town. She concealed them in her schoolbooks.

Ottar, Hans, and Irma were, respectively ten, twelve, and fifteen years old in 1943, when the first agents moved in to their home. Together with their mother, father, and grandparents, they were alone on Bjørgeholmen, situated between Ålesund and Ellingsøya. The small farm, with its six cows, a «Christmas pig», a horse, and sheep that were sent up in the mountains in summer, was an ideal hide-out. The family wished to aid the resistance movement, and their father said yes when asked if they would take in a few people for a while. It turned out to be two years, and many people.

Pistols and weapons were part of the everyday lives of the children on Bjørgeholmen. In the barn, the cases of weapons and ammunition were packed so tightly that there was hardly room for the hay, and in the living room agents went about with revolvers on their belts.

– It was often my job to polish the weapons. The only ones I wasn't allowed to touch were the hand grenades, says Ottar.

– At one time, we had enough weapons stored in the loft and buried in a grove behind the house to outfit 800 men, says Hans.

– One Christmas, we had an agent staying in the living room. Suddenly a woman from the neighbourhood knocked on the door. I hopped on the sofa with the agent and pulled the blanket over us. Mum explained that I had a boyfriend from Volda visiting, says Irma. Several years after the war she met the same woman again. "How are things going with the boyfriend from Volda?" she wanted to know.

«There were always
agents at our
farm»

Name: Dagmar Nikøy Hillersøy
Maiden name: Nikøy
Born: 18.08.1921
Place of birth: Kjøpstad in Hyllestad, Sogn and Fjordane
Residence: Bulandet in Askvoll, Sogn and Fjordane

Left for Shetland with agents who had been on a clandestine mission to Norway.

«The agents took me with them to Shetland»

Dagmar Nikøy (married name Hillersøy) was working at her aunt Kristina's café on Bulandet when they received a visit from strangers. It wasn't uncommon that fishermen and strangers came to the fishing settlement farthest out in Sunnfjord, but Dagmar Nikøy realised there was something special about these men who had taken the room in the café's loft that November day in 1941.

The two men stayed at the café several days. Dagmar Nikøy served them food and straightened their rooms, but she never asked them any questions.

– I suspected who they were and where they were from, but I didn't say a word.

Since the outbreak of war, the twenty-year-old seasonal worker, who also cooked dinner during the herring catch and stood on the processing line when the work was at its heaviest, had seen a few things on the small islands furthest west in the sea. It was here the first organised transport of fishing boats had arrived from Shetland, full of weapons and radio operators. And it was from here that her uncle, merchant Petter Nikøy, had helped many refugees over to Shetland. The 250 plus residents had more than once met people who made a habit of journeying back and forth over the North Sea.

This time it was two men from Shetlands-Larsen's own crew who were staying in the small attic room at the café. Andrew Gjertsen and Anders Merkesdal were two of the Shetland Bus fishing boat warriors who came to the Norwegian coast on secret missions. This time there had been a problem: the boat *Nordsjøen* had foundered just north of Kristiansund, where they had been placing mines. For three weeks they had been crossing snow-decked mountains and rowing from island to island to make their way to Bulandet, where they knew there was help to be had. Now they needed to find a boat so they could return to the base in Shetland.

It didn't take many days before the people at Bulandet had readied a boat, and Aunt Kristina had a serious talk with the girls at the café. She wanted both Dagmar and her cousin Hildur to accompany the agents back to Shetland. They had seen too much and their aunt knew what it could mean to have been involved in these activities. It was safer for them if they left.

– We understood that it would be best for us to leave, says Dagmar Nikøy Hillersøy from Bulandet, the island group known as Norway's westernmost fishing community.

«I considered leaving, but found I was more useful in the woods»

Name: Arne Øvrebotten
Born: 04.09.1923
Place of birth: Øvrebotten in Bremanger,
Sogn and Fjordane
Residence: Øvrebotten in Bremanger,
Sogn and Fjordane

Had regular contact with agents who came over the North Sea.

During the final years of the war, Arne Øvrebotten and his almost fifty-year-old father Torbjørn had steady contact with agents in the North Sea Traffic. On the little farm with its cattle, sheep, goats, a few hens and a «Christmas pig», the agents could sit in the «good room» with the radio operator for weeks.

Ringed with dense woods yet near the sea, the small farm in Øvrebotten outside Svelgen was ideal for developing military resistance groups. The Norwegian agents from Company Linge trained Arne Øvrebotten as a weapons instructor. Soon they had built up large contingents of armed men that trained in the mountains.

– My father often went along to collect weapons shipments from Shetland, and we contacted Shetland more than once for them to pick up people who had to get out of the country. But our most important assignment was to maintain the station for the Linge Men when they lay here during reconnaissance missions with wireless operators, says Arne Øvrebotten, who had been a central figure in the local military organisation «Milorg».

Towards war's end the German secret police Gestapo became so intrusive that Arne's father had to escape over the North Sea, while Arne moved up in the mountains with two agents and others from Milorg.

Nearly sixty years later, he makes the trip back to their hiding place in the mountain. A half hour's walk from the farm, deep in a dense forest, lies the provisional cabin constructed in the spring of 1944. The hide-out is tucked tightly under a crag and walled with grey stone, the crevices between the stones packed with moss for isolation. Turf with juniper and heather covered the roof and a pine tree was planted in front of the entryway. Here four or five individuals could lie in hiding with the radio operator, some machine guns and a bicycle-driven generator used to charge up the accumulator. After dark, his five-years-junior sister Oddbjørg would come up with food. To avoid making tracks in the snow, she had to wade in the river.

Today the cabin has caved in. Only a grey stone foundation stands as a reminder of the agents who crossed the North Sea to build up a military resistance movement in the mountain home.

– It was a tough time for our family. My mother struggled to get a hold of enough food. We sometimes had three times as many people to feed as usual. Worst was the time when the Gestapo came to the door. Arne and his father climbed out the kitchen window and took off for the mountains, while his mother and sister hastily washed the coffee cups they had used. The Gestapo turned the house over and pushed Oddbjørg in front of them through all the rooms. They confiscated a picture of his father to aid them in their search for the farmer.

– My mother was deeply affected by the war. I still wake up at night myself, re-experiencing episodes from that time. The events of the war are burned into the memory of Arne Øvrebotten.

«We had pills that would make us die»

Aslaug Ulriksen and her husband Mathias were ecstatic when the war ended. They could finally destroy the suicide pills they had concealed between the wooden beams and moss of the old stairway.

Name: Aslaug Ulriksen
Born: 27.09.1915
Maiden name: Georgsdotter
Place of birth: Barekstad on Hovden in Flora, Sogn and Fjordane
Residence: Domba on Hovden in Flora, Sogn and Fjordane

Neighbour to a much-used contact person and met many agents.

The mother of two children, Aslaug, in her twenties, and her ten-years-older husband were never directly involved in the resistance movement. Nevertheless, they knew so much that they were prepared to end their lives. Their neighbour, Martin Domben, was a frequently-used contact person for the boats that came from Shetland. Here smacks, sub-chasers, and MTB's came right into the narrow bay on which they lived. On them were agents, saboteurs, and tons of weapons and equipment. At the Domben house, the specially-trained Norwegian agents could sit for weeks at their radio transmitters while waiting for boats from Shetland.

The island Hovden, on which Domba is located, along with the other islands outside Florø, is in an area on the Norwegian coast where boats from Shetland frequently landed. Here it was easy to hide between the islands and rocks, the passage out to the sea was short, and with the almost 500-meter high mountain on Batalden as a landmark, the island was easy to find.

In Domba, the little roadless hamlet on the west side of the island, there were only two farms in addition to Martin Domben's farm. Both of these neighbours knew well what took place deep in the bay. They even assisted when needed. Mathias helped to hide some of the boxes of weapons, while Aslaug lent bedclothes when the contact man had many guests. She even cooked sour cream

porridge («rømmegrøt») for the entire crew of a torpedo boat that came from Shetland, and another time served tinned pork chops to two agents. This close contact was sufficient to expose the two neighbouring families to serious danger.

– I had been on board the Shetland Bus and knew everything. Had I revealed anything, an entire community would have been in jeopardy.

Fearful she might expose the resistance activities on the island, Aslaug refused anaesthesia when her appendix suddenly needed to be removed in all haste. She had been in hospital before and knew that people on anaesthesia spoke volumes. This she could not risk.

— My lips were ragged afterwards. Aslaug Ulriksen had defied doctors' advice and had her appendix removed without anaesthesia.

— I have often reflected upon how extraordinary it was of Martin Domben to not say a word about us when the Gestapo took him in February of 1945.

Today the unassuming woman is alone in the remote hamlet by the sea. Her neighbours gave up long ago and moved onto the mainland.

Name: Joachim Holmboe Rønneberg
Born: 30.08.1919
Place of birth: Ålesund, Møre and Romsdal
Residence: Ålesund, Møre and Romsdal

**The agent and war hero who doesn't
sit well with the role of «hero».**

Ålesunder Joachim Rønneberg is one of the most celebrated heroes of the war. Both films and books have been inspired by the operations in which he was involved. «Kampen om tungtvannet» («The Battle of the Heavy Water»), «Vinterkrig på Hardangervidda» («Winter War on Hardanger Plateau»), and «Heroes of Telemark» are all titles in which Rønneberg's exploits are featured. The events are taken from reality.

Joachim Rønneberg is the saboteur who participated in detonating the heavy water plant in Vemork; the agent who for long periods operated behind enemy lines; and the Linge-man specially trained in explosives, weapons-use, and hand-to-hand combat. Yet this man, who has received the highest distinctions from both sides of the North Sea, shies away from the role of "war hero". He shuns all forms of hero-worship and adulation.

– We weren't supermen or contemporary cowboys. I'm no hero. I was just along to carry out a mission planned by the British.

At twenty-two-years-old, he crossed the North Sea on a fishing boat. His young body pumped with adrenalin. He ached to take part in the battle. He longed for action and excitement. Little did the young Ålesunder know, he would come nearer the war than most. He would become a saboteur. In March 1943, Rønneberg was dropped by parachute over the Hardanger plateau. Together with eight other Linge-men, he blew up Norsk Hydro's electrolysis installation for heavy water, just outside of Rjukan, and got himself back to Shetland. The allies characterised the mission as the most perfectly orchestrated sabotage action in an occupied area.

The battle-hungry youth had not yet fulfilled military service when he left Norway, but in Great Britain he trained with other young men who were of the same mindset. Joachim Rønneberg learned everything about weapons and survival. What should he do if captured? Where is the best place to stab in order to kill someone with a dagger? How do you detonate a building? He even learned how to end his own life with a poisonous pill. The boys in the Linge-Company built up a self-confidence beyond compare. There was nothing they didn't feel they could handle.

– At first it seemed quite brutal; but for me, wanting to get into active service as quickly as possible, it was perfect.

The trips back and forth resulted in the agents claiming two home countries. When they were in England, they would say they were going home to Norway. As soon as they landed in Norway they began to talk about when they would head home – to England.

«It was exciting,
but we weren't
cowboys»

«Contact with the
enemy punishable by
death»

All That Remained

A bell tower, two net sheds, naked
foundations, and a few cellars.
All that remained after the Germans wreaked
their revenge in April 1942.

Televåg on Sotra, Hordaland

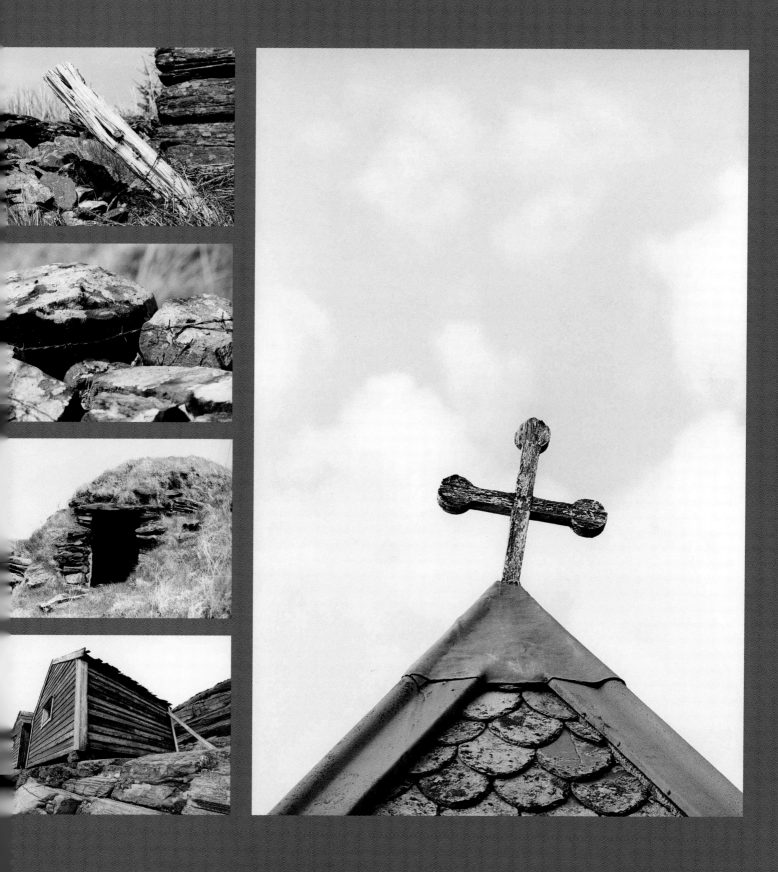

«Contact with the
enemy punishable
by death»

Name: Johannes Hillersøy
Born: 06.11.1919
Place of birth: Bulandet in Askvoll, Sogn and Fjordane
Residence: Atløy in Askvoll, Sogn and Fjordane

Taken prisoner for speaking with his brother, a member of the Shetland Bus.

Coastal fisherman Johannes Hillersøy knew it was illegal to speak to people who came over from Great Britain. He was constantly reminded of the fact by notices in the newspapers and on posters tacked up in the wheelhouses of fishing boats. «Contact with Germany's enemies will be punished by death», stood in the warnings from the German admiral.

But such warnings were of no significance when Johannes unexpectedly encountered his brother on a fishing boat not far from home. His four-years-older brother Olai had set sail from Bulandet in the direction of Shetland only six months earlier. Now he was suddenly back as a fisherman in his home waters.

– We had heard about boats coming from Shetland, but I didn't know Olai was involved in this traffic, says Johannes about the thrilling encounter on the south side of the neighbouring island Værlandet in April 1942.

As a member of the Shetland Bus, Olai Hillersøy had become one of the Germans' worst enemies. Punishment for communicating with such an enemy, even one's own brother, would be ruthless.

On 19th May 1942, Johannes Hillersøy was brutally apprehended in his home on Bulandet and led away with a revolver at his neck. For the next 18 months the 23-year-old was a German prisoner. The same fate befell his father, his two brothers, and 16 others in their community.

– It is utterly astonishing that I survived. I was beaten with large rubber clubs. I collapsed three times before we arrived at the mainland. My back was completely black and I bled under my arms, he says in a voice that reveals his discomfort with the topic.

Only after the war did he find out what had happened. After the joyous family reunion outside the islands on the perimeter of Sunnfjord, Olai Hillersøy continued to Telavåg with the two agents and the weapons shipment he had on board. But after the load was delivered and the boat had returned to Shetland, something went terribly wrong. The contact man in Telavåg had been exposed, and the Germans had surprised the little settlement. One agent was shot and the other taken prisoner before the entire community was razed to the ground.

– Our names were probably tortured out of the poor agent who survived the shooting. We had been on board the fully-laden boat and spoken with the agents before they continued on to Telavåg. That's how the Germans found their way to Bulandet.

«They took my father hostage»

«Do you know Nils Solevåg?» the new soldiers asked when they enlisted in the new Norwegian army in Scotland. The two men had been in prison on Vollan, just outside Trondheim, before escaping Norway. While in prison they had met the man with the characteristic Sunnmøre name. «That's my father's name,» Johan Solevåg replied. This is how he learned his father was sitting in prison – and that it was his fault.

«Nine people in Ålesund and the immediate area have been taken hostage by the German secret police. The seizures took place in mid-January. No further explanation as to the reasons for the arrests has been given,» appeared in the newspaper Norsk Tidend in London in February 1942.

This was not the first time the Germans had arrested the fathers of those who crossed the North Sea. It was a tactic they used to scare others considering escape. Nobody knew when or how the Germans would strike next. For 19-year-old Johan, it was like a blow to the face when he heard the news of his father's arrest. The farmer from Solavågen, south of Ålesund,

had become a hostage. He had been apprehended on his farm and set in prison as a direct result of his son's escape to England.

– It was my fault the Germans took my father. It was something I just had to live with.

The young soldier's thoughts often turned to his father. He also thought about his mother, grandparents, and the three siblings who were left to run the small farm with its four cows, six-seven sheep, and a horse. He remembers the night when, in all secrecy, he lowered his suitcase down from his window, and then told his family that he was just going out for a walk. No one knew his real destination. The next morning they discovered that both the boy and his father's fishing boat were missing. They understood the signs.

Should he have stayed home? Had his escape been worth it? he wondered in the military camp in Scotland.

When Johan came home in 1945, no one spoke of the war. Father and son knew that they had been through an arduous time. Johan had taken part in the nerve-racking mine-clearance operation in northern Norway, and his father endured five to six months in prison. This they knew. There was nothing more to say. Life went on.

Name: Johan Nils Solevåg
Born: 19.06.1922
Place of birth: Solavågen in Sula, Møre and Romsdal
Residence: Solavågen in Sula, Møre and Romsdal

The Germans imprisoned the fathers to deter others from crossing the North Sea.

Name: Åge Odd Telle
Born: 07.07.1927
Place of birth: Telavåg on Sotra, Hordaland
Residence: Telavåg on Sotra, Hordaland

Young boy who witnessed the killings that initiated the Telavåg tragedy – the worst terror of the North Sea Traffic

Fourteen-year-old Åge Telle found himself in the centre of the worst terror raid in the history of the North Sea Traffic. He remembers the shooting drama, the blood that flowed in the bedroom, the arrests, the separation from his parents, and the constant hunger in the prison camp. The young boy was only one of some 400 Telavåg residents who suffered the consequences of the contact that people in their small community on Sotra had had with Great Britain.

– My oldest brother was executed, and my mother and father were never the same after two-to-three years in captivity. Myself, I've never escaped the nightmares.

Åge, son of Martha and Laurits Telle, is speaking about the reprisals that followed when Norwegian agents from Shetland shot two high-ranking Gestapo officers. The young boy was awoken by thundering boots when the German officers stormed into the bedroom he was sharing with the agents. In a matter of minutes, he witnessed three deaths – the deaths that sparked off the Telavåg tragedy.

The Germans exacted a gruesome revenge. The settlement was to be annihilated. Every single house was dynamited or torched, the livestock removed, and the boats sunk or confiscated. All men between the ages of 16 and 60 were arrested. Most were sent to Sachsenhausen, a concentration camp. Women, children, and the elderly were interned, held prisoner for two years.

Back in the ruins of the house it all started in – the house no one could bear to restore, Åge recounts the terror he experienced as a young boy. With a shudder, he relates the story of the interrogations at the Gestapo house, the isolation and fear in the Bergen county jail, the hunger in Ulven prison camp, and the uncertainty on Framnes.

– I was always hungry. In the prison camp I consumed more pig swill than the pigs. I even ate a mocking bird shot down by the commandant.

The teenager from Telavåg found the pitiless world of death and decay oppressive. It did not get easier after the war. Then he had to endure the stares of those in the community who resented the family that had provoked the reprisals. Living in Telavåg became too difficult for Åge. He found a job in Bergen and went to sea. Only many years after the settlement had been rebuilt did he move back to Telavåg. Today, he lives only a few stone's throws from the ruins where the shooting drama took place in the early morning of 26th April, 1942. Sixty years later, the remains of his home lie as a memorial to the most devastating siege in the history of the Norwegian occupation.

«The Germans were so furious
they destroyed everything»

«We thought we were returning home»

Name: Edvard Alfred
Øvretveit
Born: 13.10.1906
Place of birth: Telavåg
on Sotra, Hordaland
Residence: Telavåg on
Sotra, Hordaland

Name: Magda Elida
Øvretveit
Maiden name: Midttveit
Born: 09.08.1912
Place of birth: Telavåg
on Sotra, Hordaland
Residence: Telavåg
on Sotra, Hordaland

They paid the price for others' freedom. She and her six children were imprisoned. He carted corpses in Sachsenhausen.

Like the other residents of Telavåg, Magda and Edvard Øvretveit were torn from their home when, in April 1942, the Germans arrived to exact their revenge. An entire community, both young and old, would pay for the North Sea Traffic that had been so active in the fishing settlement.

– We weren't going to be gone long. We were supposed to be allowed to go home again. So I took only food and a little clothing.

Magda describes the day when 268 women, children, and elderly were gathered at the youth centre in Telavåg. The oldest was 94; the youngest, twelve weeks. Magda was in her thirtieth year and had brought six children into the world. Only when they were interned in Storetveit school did she realise the truth. They would not be going home. The mother and her children had become prisoners – innocent victims for something they had not done. In their fury, the Germans razed the entire settlement to the ground.

It was distressing for the mother of six to be separated from her three oldest children while in prison, but fortunately she was not aware of the inhumane conditions Edvard was experiencing in the German concentration camp Sachsenhausen.

– We removed the dead bodies from the execution area. We used a box to carry the corpses, and set them down in front of the crematorium oven. I'll never forget the roar and the red-hot sea of fire in that oven.

Edvard describes the fear, toil, hunger, and death in the extermination camp, where a hundred thousand prisoners died of starvation, disease, exhaustion, or execution. Here it was not only the weakest who succumbed. Strong, energetic men in the prime of their lives were broken, dying in a short period of time. Of the 72 from Telavåg who were sent to German concentration camps, 31 never returned.

It wasn't long before reports of the deaths began to arrive at the prison camp in Norway. The

women of Telavåg now knew where their men were, and not a day passed that they didn't think of them. Magda lived in fear that the next message of death might be addressed to her.

Both Magda and Edvard returned to Telavåg. Back to build up their homes. Back to show that they couldn't be bested. Yet it was not to be easy.

– I don't have a night of peace, says Edvard about the hell he endured in the mortuaries of Germany.

Magda and Edvard are one of many innocent couples along the coast who had to pay for other people's freedom. For almost sixty years they have borne the invisible scars of war.

«They took all
the men»

Name: Gudrun Gjertsen
Maiden name: Myrvåg
Born: 20.05.1927
Place of birth: Værlandet in Askvoll, Sogn and Fjordane
Residence: Florø, Sogn and Fjordane

Left alone with her mother and sister after the Gestapo took all the men on the farm.

Gudrun Myrvåg (married name Gjertsen) will always remember the day the Germans came to Værlandet and took all the men on the farm. She can still see them clearly – the «pack» as she calls them. One had an exceptionally round red face. He was known as «Bloodface». The others wore long leather coats and hats. The young girl could see what kind of people they were.

– «Bloodface» locked Mamma, my sister and me in an outhouse. If we didn't keep quiet, we would taste this, he told us, showing us his revolver.

When the women in the Myrvåg family finally managed to escape the outhouse, all the men from the farm were gone. It wasn't long before they found out what had happened. Harald, Gudrun's older brother, had been beaten with an iron bar down by the boat shed, and taken prisoner along with her younger brother Sigmund. They had arrested her father, Teodor, at a town meeting in Askvoll. All were mercilessly beaten before being sent to Germany. Harald never returned, Teodor came home a broken man, and Sigmund developed severe nerve problems that left him barely able to speak. This was the punishment for having had contact with the boats from Shetland.

With the men gone, life on the farm became increasingly difficult for the women. On Værlandet, the most westward lying island group in Norway, fisherman's wife Jenny Sofie and her children sat alone with responsibility for the house and the farm. Sigrid was 16 years old, Gudrun only 14.

– It was incredibly difficult. We had to get the hay in alone and we had to go out on the boats to fish. We had food, so we didn't starve, but easy it wasn't, remembers Gudrun about life fishing and farming on the island far out in the sea.

– We knew the activity was illegal, but we never imagined the punishment would be so brutal. These memories from the war have haunted me through the years. To think that peaceful people could be taken away like that. It was unspeakable.

Siblings who escaped the reign of terror in Telavåg, but lived the entire war in fear of arrest.

Name: Marta Kristiansen
Maiden name: Telle (changed to Mortensen after Telavåg tragedy)
Born: 16.08.1924
Place of birth: Telavåg on Sotra, Hordaland
Residence: Hauglandshella on Askøy, Hordaland

Name: Anny Andora Sæle
Maiden name: Telle (changed to Mortensen after Telavåg tragedy)
Born: 30.06.1927
Place of birth: Telavåg on Sotra, Hordaland
Residence: Rong in Øygarden, Hordaland

Name: Willy Telle (changed to Mortensen after Telavåg tragedy)
Born: 15.04.1936
Place of birth: Telavåg on Sotra, Hordaland
Residence: Telavåg on Sotra, Hordaland

«We lived in hiding throughout the war»

When the Germans began to assemble the men in Telavåg, Marie Telle fled in a rowboat with the rest of her children. Her husband Johan had already departed with the youngest children. The large family were among the very few who managed to flee before the Gestapo imprisoned the remaining residents and incinerated their homes. In this manner, siblings Marta, Anny, and Willy evaded the horrible revenge that decimated an entire community; but they did not escape the anxiety. For the duration of the war they lived in fear of discovery.

– Mum and Dad didn't feel safe, and decided to go away for a few days, say the siblings, who with this turn eluded horror in a German prison.

After the shooting drama in the home of telegraph manager Laurits Telle in April 1942, the Germans began to gather some of the men – many of them fathers with sons in England. Johan Telle hadn't been involved in organising the traffic of refugees and weapons through the settlement, but he had a son in England. When the Germans left with twelve prisoners on Sunday evening, the community relaxed. Now it must be over, they thought. But Johan Telle did not relax. In the grey dawn the next morning he took the youngest children with him and rowed away in the family's boat.
Willy was only six years old, and doesn't remember much about the boat trip. Anny was fourteen and remembers more:

– Dad was terrified. All Sunday he hid out in the fields, and early Monday morning we rowed away.

We were extremely nervous and rowed in and out of all the bays for fear of being detected, says Anny.

The family split into two groups, in order to not attract attention. At home sat their mother, grandmother, and 17-year-old Marta, together with three younger brothers. Wednesday evening they stole down to the rowboat, but panicked at the sight of some Germans not far away. Early the next morning they made another attempt. Now they were in a hurry and didn't worry about the suitcases standing packed and ready in the boat house. Now their only objective was to get away. Two hours later they reached the neighbouring community of Steinsland. Here they heard that the Germans had arrested all the men and had posted a guard. No one was allowed to leave or enter the settlement. A few days later they watched the smoke from two hundred burning homes, barns, boathouses and outhouses. One of the homes was their own.

– We lived in constant fear of exposure. Every time we saw a German, we were sure they had come to arrest us.

The family dropped their characteristic Telavåg name, and began to use the name Mortensen. With this surname, Willy enrolled in school, Anny was confirmed, and their father continued as a construction worker, fisherman, and handyman. Yet concern for the relatives and neighbours who had lost their freedom was ever on their minds. The family couldn't understand how they had managed to avoid the same fate.

«Many were
forgotten»

A Memorial in Stone and Bronze

A silent group of war veterans honours a
comrade. An entire community lends its support.
The name of another war hero
is forged in stone and bronze.

From no other period in our history
do we have more
monuments.

Gamlem in Haram, Møre and Romsdal
Svortland on Bømlo, Hordaland
Ålesund, Møre and Romsdal
Scalloway, Shetland

Name: Sigfrid
Larsen Nesse
Maiden name: Nesse
Born: 20.07.1932
Place of birth: Nesse
outside Svortland
on Bømlo,
Hordaland
Residence: Nesse
outside Svortland
on Bømlo,
Hordaland

**Schoolgirl
who found it
difficult to come
home again
after the war.**

– It was difficult coming home to little Nesse outside Svortland on Bømlo. Children my age laughed at me and thought I was lying when I talked about my life in London. The war took my school years and my childhood, says Sigfrid Larsen Nesse.

When twelve-year-old Sigfrid returned home from London she told her friends about what she had seen in the big city. But the girls home on Bømlo couldn't in their wildest fantasies imagine what she was talking about. They laughed at her, called her a liar, and thought she was trying to be more important than them. That day she decided to never again speak of England.

– I don't blame them. I would certainly have behaved the same way. There was an unfathomable difference between life in Nesse and life in London.

The leap from a little fishing and farming community to one of the world's largest cities was indescribable. At Nesse there were no more than thirty houses. In all the three municipalities that today comprise Bømlo, there lived at that time under 7500 people, to London's four million. At home there was hardly a handful of cars on the roads. In London, the streets teemed with cars, huge buses, and trains that went through tunnels underground. The school she had attended there was enormous compared with the one at home.

The schoolgirl had learned many new things in the course of the three and a half years she had spent in exile. Yet she had to put her big city ways behind her when she returned to Bømlo.

– We often went to the movies, I learned a folk dance that we performed, and the girls at the school taught me how to curl my hair. But for the Christians in Nesse, all this was sinful. What had become normal for me, I couldn't even mention at home. I even had to burn the stack of cards I'd brought with me from London, remembers Sigfrid, who still dreams about life in London. The young girl from Nesse was in her first year of junior school when she had to leave the country. When she returned she was in her first year of secondary school.

– Can you imagine? Beginning in secondary school and not knowing anything. I didn't go to a school like ours at home. In London everything was different. There we learned about pounds and pence and studied other languages and we didn't have religion classes. Religion was the most important subject at home.

– I feel that the war stole my school years. I still feel bad about it, says Sigfrid Larsen Nesse outside the small house in Oldereide on Bømlo where, nine years old, she lay in hiding before escaping over the North Sea.

Only in recent years has she dared to speak about the war years, yet she still says as little as possible. Nor did she speak much with her parents about the war. As a result, she has many unanswered questions. What kind of illegal activity was her father involved in? Why did we have to flee that November evening in 1941? How did things turn out for the other forty-odd refugees who lay in hiding with them on Bømlo for over a week? Now it is too late to find answers. Those who had been with them are gone.

«I didn't dare talk about
      where I'd been»

«I didn't dare talk about
      where I'd been»

«The whisky kept us alive»

It could be excruciatingly tough during the war, but it was even worse afterwards. Einar Torvanger from Bremanger is only one of many who crossed to England who are yet haunted by nightmares and sleepless nights.

The retired fisherman and war veteran in Bremangerlandet seldom sleeps more than four hours a night. His thoughts drift back to the war, and the nightmares jar him awake. After he retired, it became even worse. Now he is alone, with all the time in the world to think about what happened during the war.

– I think constantly about the ugliness we were involved in. We fought against both bullets and storms. It wasn't exactly Sunday school.

Einar Torvanger took his father's sailboat and sailed over the North Sea in order to enlist in the military. He wanted to fight the war – and he did. Twenty-two-years-old, he began service on the Norwegian torpedo boat *MTB 627*.

– It's not a pretty topic. We shot as long as we heard voices, says the navy man about one of the boats he sank on the Norwegian coast. It is such memories that still prey upon him sixty years later.

Back in Great Britain after a demanding raid on the Norwegian coast, the boys were supposed to unwind. They usually ended up in a bar. Heavy drinking seemed to hold their problems at bay –for the time being.

– The alcohol kept us alive. This is what the doctors told us after the war.

Home again, Einar Torvanger is only one of many for whom the excitement and battle-thirst of the war re-emerged as nightmares and other afflictions. He was to be reminded of this every single day.

Name: Einar Torvanger
Born: 21.11.1921
Place of birth: Torvanger
in Bremanger,
Sogn and Fjordane
Residence: Igland
in Bremanger,
Sogn and Fjordane

One of many in the England Crossing who still struggle with nightmares and sleepless nights.

«We never received
acknowledgement»

Name: Ingeborg Skagenes
Maiden name: Skagenes
Born: 12.02.1925
Place of birth: Skageneset on Radøy, Hordaland
Residence: Manger on Radøy, Hordaland

One of many resisters who were overlooked after the war.

Ingeborg Skagenes must be one of the most courageous resisters on the entire Norwegian coast. Nevertheless, she was forgotten at war's end.

Only seventeen years old, Ingeborg regularly met refugees who arrived by the coastal boat at Manger pier – north of Bergen. Unafraid, she smiled and waved at the Germans along the quay as she rowed by with boatloads of refugees – and the Germans blew kisses back at her. With up to five or six refugees in her boat, she rowed the hour-long journey home to her mother on the remote farm Skageneset. There the refugees received food and shelter for a few days or weeks, before they were smuggled further by others to the Shetland Buses and to freedom on the other side of the North Sea.

– Of course we were frightened, but we felt we had to help.

After the war, Ingeborg, her mother Dorthea, her sister Eva, and her brother Nils were forgotten. While the authorities awarded medals to heroes in uniform, the little family at Skageneset received not so much as a thank-you. Compensation or remuneration were never mentioned. It was not until 52 years later that official Norway discovered the unique contribution made by the women and children of Skageneset during the war. Then came diplomats, a medal from the Ministry of Defence, and laudatory speeches. Ingeborg's mother was unable to enjoy this recognition; she had been dead for 23 years.

– We didn't help the refugees for money or praise. This was never in our thoughts, says Ingeborg. She is back in the little cottage that they moved away from a few years after the war. Up to thirteen refugees at a time might be stretched out on their floor. Only after darkness had fallen could the strangers step outside for fresh air. Today, Ingeborg cannot comprehend how they managed to shelter so many people.

Some of their neighbours thought the family had grown wealthy from their resistance work. One man was so envious after the war that he beat up the youngest brother, Nils, for having «endangered the entire community».

The modest family was far from wealthy. The truth was nearer the opposite. After Ingeborg's father died in 1941, only her mother and three teenagers were left on the outlying island. They lived off the little farm with its two cows, a pig, some sheep, and hens. This was just enough for their family of four. Miraculously, and without any contributions from others, they nonetheless managed to feed around eighty refugees. Yet after the war, the family was destitute. Their reserve capital had been depleted; the money they could have used on themselves had been used on people they didn't know. Besides materials from some old German barracks, the Samaritans on Skageneset received no remuneration.

– Someone once asked if we had received compensation or an award. Yes, my mother replied. We received a free country.

*Name: Barbara Elspeth Mary Melkevik
(changed her name from Olsen to Melkevik
in Norway)
Maiden name: Christie
Born: 08.12.1925
Place of birth: Scalloway, Shetland
Residence: Klokkarvik on Sotra, Hordaland*

Shetland woman who moved to Norway after the war.

Sixty years after the occupation, Barbara Melkevik is alone in the coastal landscape on Sotra outside of Bergen. She is one of the Shetland girls who lost her heart to a Norwegian soldier, married, and moved to Norway. Now the man who brought her to this country is gone, and Barbara is alone in a foreign country – just as many Norwegian women were when they were on the other side during the war.

– When my husband died, people thought I would move back to Shetland. But I had lived fifty years here in this country. Norway had become my native country.

Barbara has strong roots in Norway now. She has brought five children into the world and passes her time with her 15 grandchildren and 18 great-grandchildren. The woman from Shetland even speaks a fluent coastal dialect. It hasn't always been like this. She remembers how difficult it was to learn the language, but there was no other way. Her husband, Arne Olsen Melkevik, had hung up his navy uniform from the Shetland Bus and returned to his work as a fisherman and seaman.

This meant that the 19-year-old mother was often alone in a country where almost nobody spoke English.

– I said to myself: «Barbara – if you are going to live here you must learn the language.»

Barbara wandered through stores and markets listening to how people spoke, and soon she could make herself understood. It was harder to leave the people she knew: her friends and family in Scalloway. In Norway, she threw herself into her role of housewife and mother, and as a result never had time to develop the kind of close relationships she had enjoyed in Shetland. This is something she regrets now that she is alone again.

When Barbara met the blonde navy sailor from Norway, she never considered how much her life would change. She worked at the hotel where the men ate. He was a soldier in her village. From the evening he accompanied her home, it was her heart that took control. Not long afterwards, he appeared with a gold ring from Aberdeen, and in January 1944 he placed the wedding ring on her right ring finger – as was the custom in Norway.

– Many of the other brides from Shetland moved back when they were left alone, but for me this was not an option. I am Norwegian now – both in my heart and on paper.

«I met a soldier and
became Norwegian»

«I met a soldier and
became Norwegian»

«They were forgotten after the war»

– After the war, those who had crossed to England were forgotten. Quietly and unnoticed, they returned to anonymity – just as they had been before they crossed the North Sea. They were neither heroes nor villains. They simply continued their lives as if nothing had happened.

Name: Ragnar Leif Ulstein
Born: 19.04.1920
Place of birth: Ulstein
on Sunnmøre,
Møre and Romsdal
Residence: Ålesund,
Møre and Romsdal

Hardly anyone knows the story of the people who crossed to England and the North Sea Traffic better than journalist and author Ragnar Ulstein. The Sunnmøre man had himself crossed over, and was one of the Linge agents who travelled back and forth over the North Sea.

Early in the 1960's, twenty years after thousands of young men and women made their way over the North Sea, he interviewed 250 of these individuals. His assignment was to write the story of the England Crossing. This is how he describes the people he met at that time:

Journalist and author who brought the Norwegians who had crossed to England back from oblivion.

«They were ordinary tax-payers, lacking any special status in their communities. They were anonymous people focused on healing their wounds and continuing their everyday lives. They had not spoken about what they had been involved in, and they had made no demands of any sort.»

Along the entire coast the journalist encountered people who could not understand why their stories held any interest for others. Yet the anonymous war heroes had more than thrilling war stories to narrate. Many of them had become war-invalids. Ragnar Ulstein met individual after individual struggling with painful memories and an ungrateful bureaucracy. These ordinary people who had fought for Norway were not merely forgotten – many of them were in strenuous situations. Obtaining social support, retirement pensions, and compensation were only a few of the problems they dealt with. With 700 pages

of history and a long series of articles in the newspaper *Bergens Tidende*, Ragnar Ulstein called an entire nation's attention to the plight of the neglected sojourners.

– I was given the role of a rescuer. I travelled around and rescued people from oblivion. I have continued this work for almost forty years now, says the author, who has more than ten books about the war to his credit.

In contrast to all the heroic tales that surfaced just after the war, Ragnar Ulstein's stories focussed on ordinary men and women living along the entire Norwegian coast. The coastal dwellers who stood up and fought back – because they believed it was the right thing to do.

The visible scars in the landscape were gone,

but the furrows in the faces of the coastal people

still had a story to tell.

Glossary

Abwehr: The German military intelligence service.

Agent: A soldier specially trained by the Linge Company – usually radio operators or saboteurs. Most of them were recruited by SOE or SIS.

Antrum: Code name for a military resistance organisation in Ålesund and the surrounding area. Radio operators were of particular importance.

England Crossing: Designation for the approximately 300 civilian boats and 3300 people who crossed over the North Sea from Norway's west coast during the war.

Export: Activities aiding refugees in their escape.

Home Forces: The military division of the Home Front, also called Milorg.

I-office: Office for Intelligence Operations. Responsible for collecting information about the occupiers and NS-activities in Norway.

Linge, Martin: (1894-1941). Actor and resistance worker. Trained a special Norwegian military force in England – the Linge Company – in collaboration with the SOE. The Linge soldiers were sent on special missions to Norway. Linge was killed during the Måløy raid in July 1941.

MTB: Motor torpedo boat. A unit of these boats was stationed in Lerwick, Shetland during the war. Their primary objective was to attack German ships along the Norwegian coast, but they were also used to transport agents and equipment.

North Sea Traffic: The North Sea connection between Great Britain and Norway during five years of war. Encompasses both the civilian passage (the England Crossing) and the military traffic that was chiefly conducted by the Shetland Bus and the crew at the SIS base in Peterhead, Scotland.

Polar Bear: SOE-operation, the goal of which was to protect the Norwegian infrastructure from German reprisals in the event of a German capitulation and retreat. Based on German destruction after the Allied invasion of Normandy.

Quisling, Vidkun: (1887-1945). Founder of the National Assembly and its leader from 1933. Hitler's man in Norway, led a coup d'état on the evening of 9th April 1940. Executed as a traitor at Akershus on 24th October 1945.

Rinnan, Henry Oliver: (1915-1947). The German's highest-ranking Gestapo agent in Norway. Executed in 1947.

Royal Victoria Patriotic School: (or, Patriotic School) Site in London at which refugees were interrogated by British authorities.

Shetland Bus: Norwegian fishermen and seamen who transported agents and military equipment from Shetland to Norway, and refugees in the other direction. At first they used fishing boats, later advancing to submarine chasers.

Shetlands-Larsen
Leif Andreas Larsen (1906-1991). Best known of the Shetland Bus skippers. Crossed the North Sea 52 times. Larsen was the highest decorated naval officer of the Second World War.

SIS: Secret Intelligence Service (MI-6). British secret intelligence service for foreign operations.

SOE: The Special Operations Executive. British secret service which conducted sabotage and subversion in Nazi-occupied areas.

Sten gun: British 9 mm machine gun. Issued to the resistance movement in Norway and several other countries.

Submarine chaser (sub-chaser): Naval vessel usually used to hunt submarines. Three of these boats were converted and given to the Shetland Bus by the American navy in 1943. As a result, the Shetland Bus could continue its transport of agents, military equipment and refugees after the fishing boats had played out their role. The three boats were dubbed the *Hessa*, the *Hitra*, and the *Vigra*.

Tirpitz: German battleship. Arrived in Norway in January 1942. A grave danger for the convoys to Murmansk, responsible for keeping extensive British flotillas engaged on the northern front. The British made several attempts to disable the ship. Not until November 1944 did they manage to sink it.

Vestige I: British SOE-operation carried out by Norwegian Linge-agents in September 1943. The operation's objective was the sinking of German ships in the Nordgulen area in Sogn and Fjordane. Only partly successful.

Work service: (AT) Before the war, an organisation for volunteer physical labour useful to the community, eg, building roads, digging ditches, clearing fields, etc. During the war, AT came under the control of the National Assembly, and was increasingly militarised. The service was also opened to women. Norway's expatriate government in London gave orders to shun the AT, and in 1944 a slew of AT files were destroyed by the resistance movement for fear that AT-members might be sent into battle on the German side of the Eastern Front.

Register of Names

Register of Places

AK Akershus, Norway

D Germany

GB Great Britain

HO Hordaland, Norway

IND India

IS Iceland

MR Møre and Romsdal, Norway

NO Nordland, Norway

NT Nord-Trøndelag, Norway

OP Oppland, Norway

OS Oslo, Norway

RO Rogaland, Norway

SF Sogn and Fjordane, Norway

ST Sør-Trøndelag, Norway

TE Telemark, Norway

TR Troms, Norway

The place-names found in this book correspond with modern usage rather than earlier designations. Consequently, not all are historically accurate, but can be located on contemporary maps.

List of Illustrations

p. 22 Shetland Museum

p. 23 Scalloway Museum

p. 24 Top: Norwegian North Sea Traffic Museum (Nordsjøfartmuseet)

p. 25 Top: Ralf Jonassen / Bergen City Archives

p. 31 Norwegian Resistance Museum (Norges Hjemmefrontmuseum)

p. 81 Norwegian Resistance Museum (Norges Hjemmefrontmuseum)

p. 106 The New Shetlander

p. 115 Imperial War Museum, London

p. 131 Sunnhordland Folkemuseum

p. 148 Aalesunds Museum

p. 151 Norwegian North Sea Traffic Museum (Nordsjøfartmuseet)

p. 167 Norwegian North Sea Traffic Museum (Nordsjøfartmuseet)

All others, older photographs: Private / Norwegian North Sea Traffic Museum (Nordsjøfartmuseet)
All others, newer photographs: Trygve Sørvaag

This book was made possible with the support of:

Ada and Hagbart Waage's Humanitarian and Charitable Foundation (Ada og Hagbart Waages humanitære og veldedige stiftelse)

The Non-fiction Literature Fund (Det faglitterære fond)

The G.C. Rieber Foundation (G.C. Rieber Fondene)

The Norwegian North Sea Traffic Museum (Nordsjøfartmuseet)

The Norwegian Council for Cultural Affairs (Norsk Kulturråd)

The Naval Society (Sjømilitære Samfund)

The Shetland Norwegian Friendship Society (Vennskapsforeininga Norge-Shetland)

Askvoll Municipality

Bømlo Municipality

Fjell Municipality

Flora Municipality

Haram Municipality

Hareid Municipality

Haugesund Municipality

Hordaland County

Sund Municipality

Øygarden Municipality

Ålesund Municipality

Bremnes Fryseri

Østensjø Shipping AS (Østensjø Rederi)

Norwick

Unst

Yell

Mid-Yell

Lunna
Vidlin
Weisdale *Whalsay*

SHETLAND ISLANDS

Scalloway LERWICK
Burra Isle

Sumburgh Head

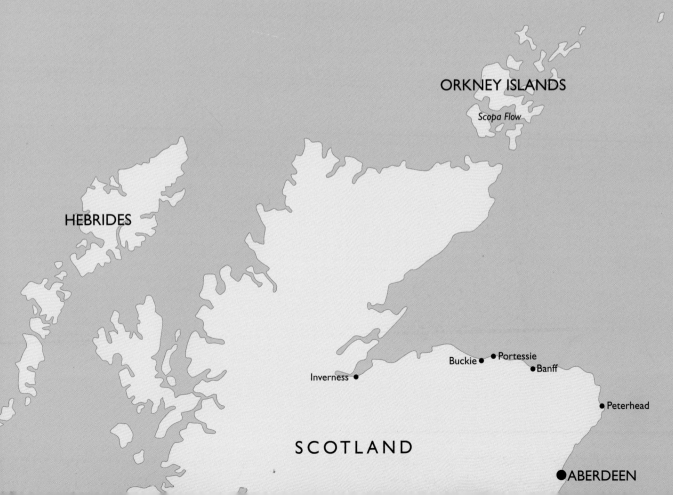

ORKNEY ISLANDS

Scopa Flow

HEBRIDES

Buckie Portessie
Banff
Inverness

Peterhead

SCOTLAND

ABERDEEN